BOLD and BRIGHT

BOLD AND BRIGHT

CHIC AND EXUBERANT INTERIOR INSPIRATION FROM BRAZIL

MAÍRA S TEIXEIRA

With an introduction by Beta Germano of *Casa Vogue Brasil*

Photography by MAÍRA ACAYABA

RYLAND PETERS & SMALL
LONDON • NEW YORK

Senior designer Toni Kay
Senior commissioning editor
Annabel Morgan
Head of production
Patricia Harrington
Art director Leslie Harrington
Editorial director Julia Charles
Publisher Cindy Richards

First published in 2016 by
Ryland Peters & Small
20–21 Jockey's Fields,
London WC1R 4BW
and
341 East 116th Street
New York, NY 10029
www.rylandpeters.com

Text copyright © Maíra Teixeira 2016
Design and photographs copyright
© Ryland Peters & Small 2016
10 9 8 7 6 5 4 3 2 1

ISBN 978-1-84975-756-0

A CIP record for this book is available
from the British Library.
Library of Congress CIP data has been
applied for.

Printed and bound in China

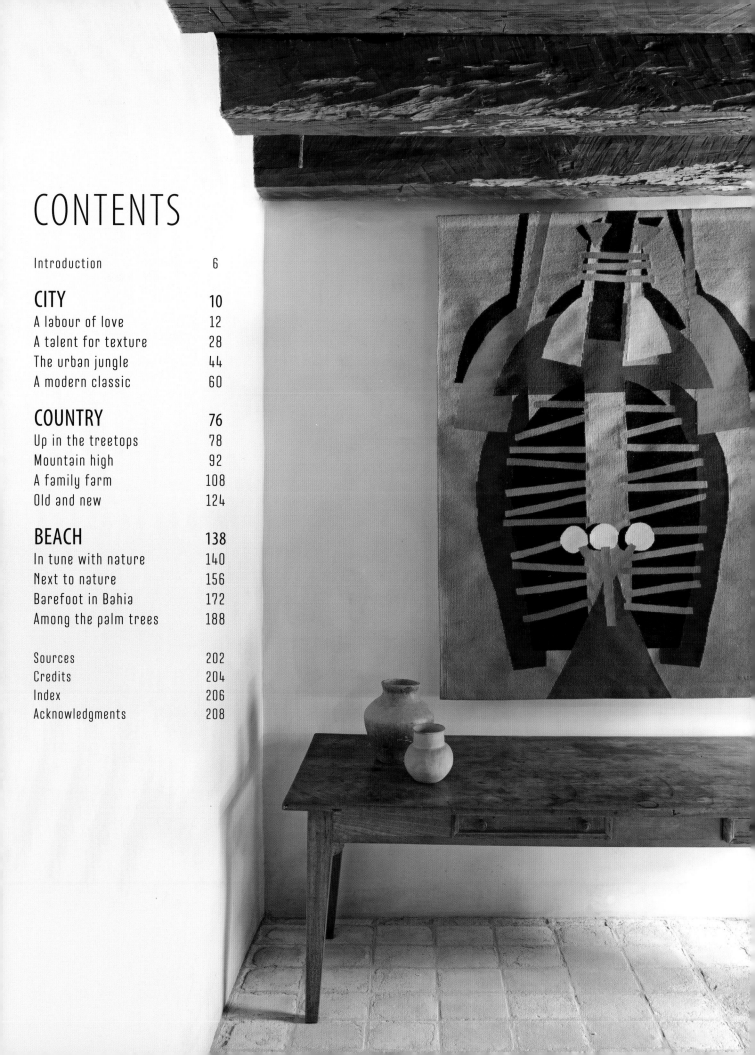

CONTENTS

INTRODUCTION

As yet relatively undiscovered in many parts of the world, Brazilian interiors have a verve, sophistication and confidence that lifts the spirits and appeals to the eye. The homes featured in this book display all the vibrant personality of the region and their use of exuberant colour, design and pattern is life enhancing. Brazilians are a naturally expansive people, and we love open spaces, high ceilings and plenty of natural light. Our homes showcase the natural materials that are in such generous supply here – rough-hewn or polished stone and a wealth of exotic hardwoods. These elements are combined with minimalist lines and sleek contemporary glamour, which provide a backdrop for carefully chosen handmade or indigenous artefacts.

Brazilian interiors also display an appreciation for pieces with soul, and therefore vintage furniture plays a starring role, as well as modern pieces made from reclaimed or sustainably grown wood. Our tropical DNA is evident in our use of colour – entire walls are given over to vivid turquoises and oranges, while occasional splashes of colour make an appearance in even the most neutral schemes. There is great interest in ecological concerns, and many of the projects in this book, such as the beach houses on pages 138–187, were designed to respect local flora and fauna. Brazil also possesses a rich colonial heritage and the Fazenda Vargem Grande (pages 124–137) and the converted barn at Monte Alegre (pages 108–123) pay tribute to the days of Brazil's coffee boom.

Finally, an abundance of lush vegetation and the pleasant climate provide a backdrop to Brazilian daily life. Our homes exploit these natural assets; almost every house in this book features outdoor living space as well as an exterior kitchen or cooking area, and this sense of connection to nature is at the very heart of the Brazilian lifestyle.

CITY

BRAZIL IS HOME TO MANY CITIES, EACH WITH ITS
OWN DISTINCT PERSONALITY AND REPUTATION. RIO
DE JANEIRO IS ASSOCIATED WITH BEACH CULTURE
AND LAID-BACK CHARM, ENERGETIC SÃO PAULO IS
BRAZIL'S BUSINESS HUB, FAMED FOR ITS FOOD SCENE
AND CULTURAL LIFE, AND ELEGANT BRASILIA IS
CELEBRATED FOR ITS UTOPIAN CITY PLAN AND
MODERNIST ARCHITECTURE. CITY HOMES IN BRAZIL
DISPLAY ALL THE GLAMOUR, PLAYFUL EXUBERANCE
AND PANACHE THAT THE COUNTRY IS FAMOUS FOR.

A LABOUR OF LOVE

Fabiana Zanin was looking for a fresh start. Out apartment hunting, she fell in love with this 150 sq m/1615 sq ft apartment on the third floor of a renowned 1940s modernist apartment block, the Edifício Louveira, which offers dazzling views over São Paulo's Higienópolis district. This affluent neighbourhood is dotted with leafy parks, cultural institutions, elegant 19th-century architecture and glossy modern apartment blocks. Unusually for São Paulo, most amenities are within walking distance, and this appealed greatly to Fabiana. 'I go everywhere on foot,' she laughs. 'My car never leaves the garage!'.

OPPOSITE *Fabiana loves cooking and entertaining, and when she renovated the apartment, the kitchen was integrated into the living area so that it would be at the heart of the home.*

ABOVE *The Edifício Louveira is located in front of Vilaboim Square in Higienópolis, São Paulo. It was designed in 1946 by Brazilian architects João Batista Vilanova Artigas and Carlos Cascaldi, and is considered an important representative of modern architecture in the city.*

Despite its stunning views, the apartment itself was tired and faded. It had last been refurbished in the 1980s and was in need of a complete overhaul. But Fabiana was undeterred. Her job as a designer allowed her to see the potential of the space and she enlisted the help of architect Flavio Miranda of Estúdio FM and designer Marcelo Rosenbaum to help her restore the apartment to its former glory.

The renovations were extensive and took a year to complete: the electrical system and other amenities were upgraded, the living room was integrated with the kitchen and existing surfaces were stripped

ABOVE Fabiana's apartment is adorned with artefacts brought back from her many travels. They add interest and detail to the neutral shades and natural textures in the living area.

LEFT Four plates forming the word AMOR (love) line up above the doorway; the font was developed by Fabiana for the A Gente Transforma project in partnership with designer Marcelo Rosenbaum. The carved wooden angel came from the north-eastern state of Piauí and the lighting is by Flavio Miranda.

OPPOSITE ABOVE The work surface around the sink is made from Corian and the chunky wooden shelves hold Fabiana's spices and groceries. The KitchenAid refrigerator can be concealed behind a chalkboard sliding door.

OPPOSITE BELOW The large island unit that separates the kitchen from the living area is made from sleek freijó wood and MDF. The raw concrete pillars offer a contrast in texture.

back to reveal exposed concrete pillars,
bare brick walls and a burned cement floor.
When it came to the décor, Fabiana opted for
neutral colours so as not to complete with
the clean modernist lines of the apartment
and in order to provide a simple backdrop
for her furniture and treasured possessions.

In the living area, the concrete floors
are covered with a huge natural fibre rug
woven by craftsmen in Brazil's historic Piauí
region. The Edifício Louveira is surrounded
by mature trees, earning the block the
nickname 'The Treehouse', and in this space
the vast 12-m/40-ft windows showcase an
ever-changing panorama of moving branches
and rustling green leaves.

ABOVE LEFT AND RIGHT *The kitchen island was made by a local carpenter and incorporates a built-in hob/stovetop at one end plus a large slab of granite that functions as a food preparation area. The huge hand-crafted spoons are not purely decorative – Fabiana uses them to cook with every day.*

RIGHT *A view from the kitchen to the dining area shows the green treetops beyond and explains why the Edifício Louveira has earned the nickname 'The Treehouse'.*

OPPOSITE *Tucked behind the dining table, built-in storage holds Fabiana's tableware: an eclectic collection ranging from pepper pots to cake stands and silver coffeepots. Sliding wooden doors conceal the shelves when desired.*

THIS PAGE *A key feature of the Edifício Louveira are the extensive floor-to-ceiling windows. As the building is now listed as being of special architectural interest, they cannot be altered or removed.*

Eating well is very important to Fabiana, and the spacious, well-equipped kitchen area is at the heart of her home. She is an excellent cook, with vegan dishes her speciality, and loves to entertain, inviting friends over for supper most nights. The focal point of the kitchen is the long island unit, designed by a local carpenter, with its elegant freijó wood and granite top and capacious green MDF cabinets below. On the wall behind, a chalkboard sliding door can be pulled across to either conceal the huge, gleaming refrigerator or the entrance to the bedrooms. In the sink area, simple white subway tiles cover the wall, the sleek work surface is made from Corian and the thick wooden shelves above house an array of spices and other culinary essentials.

Adjacent to the kitchen is the dining area. Fabiana discovered the unusual dining table and iron benches at Studio Gloria, a local store that specializes in restoring

LEFT *This light-filled corner at one end of the living area is the perfect spot for relaxation and meditation, with a traditional Brazilian hammock providing the ideal vehicle for reading or taking an afternoon nap.*

ABOVE *Fabiana loves houseplants and has many of them dotted around the apartment. They flourish in this light, bright space and seem to merge with the green treetops just outside the windows.*

RIGHT *The apartment contains an array of traditional Brazilian handicrafts alongside souvenirs and artworks that Fabiana has brought back from her travels.*

OPPOSITE *At the other end of the living area from the kitchen is Fabiana's library. The chunky shelves are stacked with books and objects picked up on her widespread travels. The handwoven natural fibre rugs that cover the floor come from the village of Várzea Queimada in the Brazilian state of Piauí.*

LEFT *The small lobby is painted a dramatic velvety matt black that contrasts with the white walls elsewhere in the apartment.*

BELOW *This unusual mid-century polished wood piece was originally used as a drinks cabinet, with glasses stored below and bottles above. It now resides in Fabiana's bedroom and holds her jewellery and other accessories.*

vintage furniture. The sliding wooden screen doors running behind the table were Fabiana's idea – like the chalkboard panel in the kitchen area, the doors can slide across to either conceal or reveal the cabinets and shelving behind, where she displays her most treasured possessions.

In the calm, understated master bedroom, the floor-to-ceiling windows allow light to flood in. The only splash of colour comes in the form of an upholstered headboard covered with vibrant Moroccan fabric purchased on one of Fabiana's trips overseas. She found the curvy wooden armchair beneath the window closer to home – at the well-known Praça Benedito Calixto flea market in São Paulo.

OPPOSITE *The guest bathroom represents a departure from the simple white walls that feature elsewhere. For this space, Fabiana selected glossy plaster-pink subway tiles that perfectly complement the copper piping taps/ faucets and the shower.*

THIS PAGE *Fabiana's bedroom is a calm and tranquil space. The large windows allow natural light to enter and the green treetops outside are a soothing sight. The headboard is upholstered in a vibrant Moroccan fabric.*

LEFT *In the master bathroom, twin sinks are positioned beneath the wide window. The taps/faucets were constructed from industrial copper piping. Through the windows can be seen the sliding yellow shutters that are a feature of the exterior of the iconic Edifício Louveira building.*

BELOW AND OPPOSITE ABOVE
The long, floating unit that holds the sinks runs the width of the window and was designed by architect Flávio Miranda. At one end, a cluster of ornamental vintage tins and jars holds Fabiana's makeup and perfumes.

OPPOSITE BELOW LEFT *In the spacious shower, industrial copper piping has again been used, in this case to create a sinuous, curving towel rail.*

Next door, the bright, white master bathroom is simple yet luxurious. Designed by architect Flávio Miranda, it features deep double sinks with taps/faucets and towel rails fashioned from industrial copper piping.

Fabiana has poured heart and soul into this renovation project and it shows. The apartment is faithful both to the historic building it inhabits and to Fabiana's vision of her ideal home. As a result, it now has a warm and welcoming personality of its own.

BELOW *At the entrance to the master bathroom, deep shelves are lined with white ceramic tiles and display books, perfumes and ornamental boxes. These personal touches soften the pared-back industrial aesthetic of the bathroom.*

A TALENT FOR TEXTURE

When architect and interior designer Julliana Camargo first visited the apartment that was to become her home, she was able to look beyond the floor plan and see that the double-height ceiling, tall windows and the absence of support beams in the middle of the space would allow her the freedom to make the perfect family home for herself, her husband and their two young daughters. Confident when it came to designing and building for others, now it was Julliana's turn to create her own interior. It took her a year to transform the original bare space into a comfortable abode, and four years later, she says, modestly, 'With time, things are taking shape.'

RIGHT *Julliana's talent for combining different textures brings this home to life. The stone for the exposed feature wall came from the Brazilian state of Minas Gerais. The right angles of the rough wooden stair treads contrast pleasingly with the organic forms of the smooth ceramic vessels by Jonathan Adler.*

OPPOSITE AND BELOW *Each and every element of the apartment was meticulously planned by Julliana to suit her family and their lifestyle. The sleek fitted kitchen is neatly stowed away in a lower-ceilinged space to one side of the double-height living area. Large cupboards with sliding doors conceal all the usual kitchen paraphernalia.*

BELOW RIGHT *At the far side of the living area, large sliding doors pull across to reveal a blue corridor that leads to the bedrooms.*

Julliana and her family live in the attractive neighbourhood of Campo Belo, in the southern part of São Paulo. This pleasant, leafy district is popular with families and originally grew up around the old town of Santo Amaro, which dates back to the early 20th century. The purchase of the apartment was, of course, a joint decision, but when it came to designing her new home, Julliana had a free rein. Her husband had just one request: a round dining table. His absolute trust in her gave Julliana the opportunity to use her creativity and skills as an architect without being bound by too many impositions.

Upon entering the apartment, a large artwork in a playful, naïve style by Brazilian artist Rita Wainer greets visitors. Beyond here, you step into a soaring double-height living space with tall windows, where a mix of bold colours, bright daylight and modern furniture set the tone for a

THIS PAGE *The white sliding doors at one end of the living room can be pulled aside to reveal the vibrant blue of the bedroom corridor, thus completely transforming the entire feel of the interior. The retro-style lime chairs pop against the azure backdrop.*

LEFT AND ABOVE *The Silver Lake armchairs were designed by Patricia Urquiola for Italian furniture company Moroso, inspired by 1950s Californian modernism. Their punchy lime hue and blocky silhouettes add colour and form to a quiet seating area. The Kartell La Boheme low stool doubles as a side table.*

BELOW *Floor-to-ceiling gauze curtains/drapes pull across the double-height windows to filter the powerful sun.*

relaxed yet luxurious family home. Texture is key and brings atmosphere and a sense of intimacy to a space that is in effect a single large cube. The wooden floors that run throughout the apartment, for example, were salvaged from a demolished house in Paraná, just to the south of São Paulo, and have a beautiful, rich patina, while the back wall of the imposing open-plan living area is clad in rough stone that Julliana sourced from the state of Minas Gerais, renowned for its geological riches.

The challenge for the open-plan living space was to create a staircase to the mezzanine level that did not take up too much space. The simple cantilevered reclaimed wood and concrete steps set into the stone wall were an ingenious solution – the stairs not only offer access to the higher level but also contribute another rich texture to the interior.

THIS PAGE *The broad terrace is home to an assortment of potted plants of all shapes and sizes, providing privacy and creating a leafy vista for the sitting room.*

It is evident that everything here was meticulously planned and chosen by Julliana: 'You go searching, and you start finding,' she says. The furniture was mostly hand-picked from a supplier who, during the course of the renovations, became a great friend. Some pieces were brought to the apartment for a photo shoot for a local magazine and never left. Others were inherited from Julliana's family, including the clay pots that hold plants in the living room and the ornate crocheted lace bedspread that adorns the couple's bed.

PREVIOUS PAGE, OPPOSITE AND THIS PAGE *The soaring white walls of the apartment offer a perfect gallery-style backdrop for the varied collection of Brazilian art, crafts and artefacts that Julliana and her husband have collected over the years.*

LEFT *The open wooden staircase leads up to the mezzanine level, which has a glass balustrade and is suspended from the ceiling by metal cables. This area is equipped with an oversized squashy sofa where the family gather to watch TV and films on the home cinema system.*

BELOW *The little girls' bedrooms are decorated with pastel shades and have a playful charm. In her younger daughter's room, Julliana opted to part-paint the walls in a chalky pale grey shade. Vibrant pops of pink and colourful toys enliven the soothing scheme.*

OPPOSITE *For her older daughter's room, Julliana designed this versatile storage unit with brightly coloured doors in different pastel shades. Toys can be tidied away quickly with just a few favourites left out on display. On the opposite wall, narrow ledge shelves fixed at child height hold a colourful selection of picture books. In the centre of the room, a large rug softens the wooden flooring and offers plenty of play space. The light fitting is Tord Boontje's Midsummer, made from die-cut tyvek.*

The most favoured spot in this home is the deep balcony leading off the living room, which is home to a large collection of tropical potted plants. Here, family meals take place at another round table, the children play and Julliana's husband relaxes and reads the papers sitting on the regal Shadowy armchair by Tord Boontje – a gift from Julliana.

All along one side of the living area, sliding white doors pull across to reveal a vibrant cobalt blue corridor that leads to the bedrooms. These rooms are tranquil and cosy, with the dark reclaimed wood floor extending even into the bathroom suites. The master bedroom is decorated in calming tones of white and chalky grey. This restful colour scheme extends into the children's rooms, where rag rugs line the floors and additional elements of pastel colour provide a contrast to the bolder shades used elsewhere.

Julliana set out to create a home full of warmth and comfort, and she has certainly achieved her aim. Her home may occupy the eighth floor of a modern block, but it is so cleverly designed that it feels more like a house. Carefully chosen natural materials provide interest, while the furniture and decorative objects strike a sophisticated yet light-hearted note. Over the years, Julliana has added various paintings and objects, yet the atmosphere remains the same: a happy family home.

ABOVE *In the master bedroom, the bed is adorned with a delicate hand-crocheted bedspread that was given to Julliana by her mother. The broad headboard is dressed with a simple cream cotton loose cover.*

ABOVE AND RIGHT *Tucked away in a narrow corner of the master bedroom is a compact home office area. Lightweight grey curtains/ drapes screen the São Paulo sun.*

ABOVE RIGHT AND FAR RIGHT *In this tiny jewel box of a cloakroom, the dramatic stone sink is hewn from a single piece of rock. It came from the same quarry in Minas Gerais as the stones on the feature walls in the main living space.*

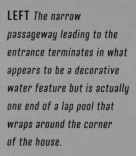

LEFT *The narrow passageway leading to the entrance terminates in what appears to be a decorative water feature but is actually one end of a lap pool that wraps around the corner of the house.*

ABOVE *The entryway is illuminated by a circular skylight. Huge doors of American oak swing open to provide a dramatic entrance.*

THE URBAN JUNGLE

Originally designed and built in 1970 by Italian–Brazilian architect Ugo di Pace, this São Paulo home was given a completely new lease of life by the architect Arthur Casas. His brief was to transform the house into a stylish contemporary home that reflected the lifestyle of its owners: empty nesters who enjoy cinema, entertaining and sport. Accordingly, one side of the narrow, rectangular plot is devoted to a 20 m/65 ft marble-lined lap pool, which offers a dramatic mirror image of the vertical gardens that border it. Keeping fit is taken seriously in this home; the couple's bedroom is accessed via their gym where they work out at home.

The house is located in the low-rise suburb of Jardins, which provides a welcome splash of greenery in the sea of skyscrapers that make up the centre of São Paulo. As part of the renovations, the original façade of the house was covered with slatted wooden screening reminiscent of *moucharabieh* – the carved wooden latticework employed in traditional Arabic architecture. The screening is shaped into a rippling wave-like formation that conceals the original robust concrete frontage and was designed to 'impart a smooth, organic movement', says the architect.

The entrance to the house is via a small passageway running alongside the house and terminating in a narrow pool that reflects the lush, tropical planting covering the boundary walls of the property.

THIS PAGE *The owners of this sleek contemporary home enjoy socializing, so when it came to renovating the house, spacious areas for entertaining were top of their wish list. With several different seating areas, the sitting room is perfect for parties. The olive green armchairs with brass legs are Marco Zanuso originals from 1955, while the free-form sofa is by Vladimir Kagan.*

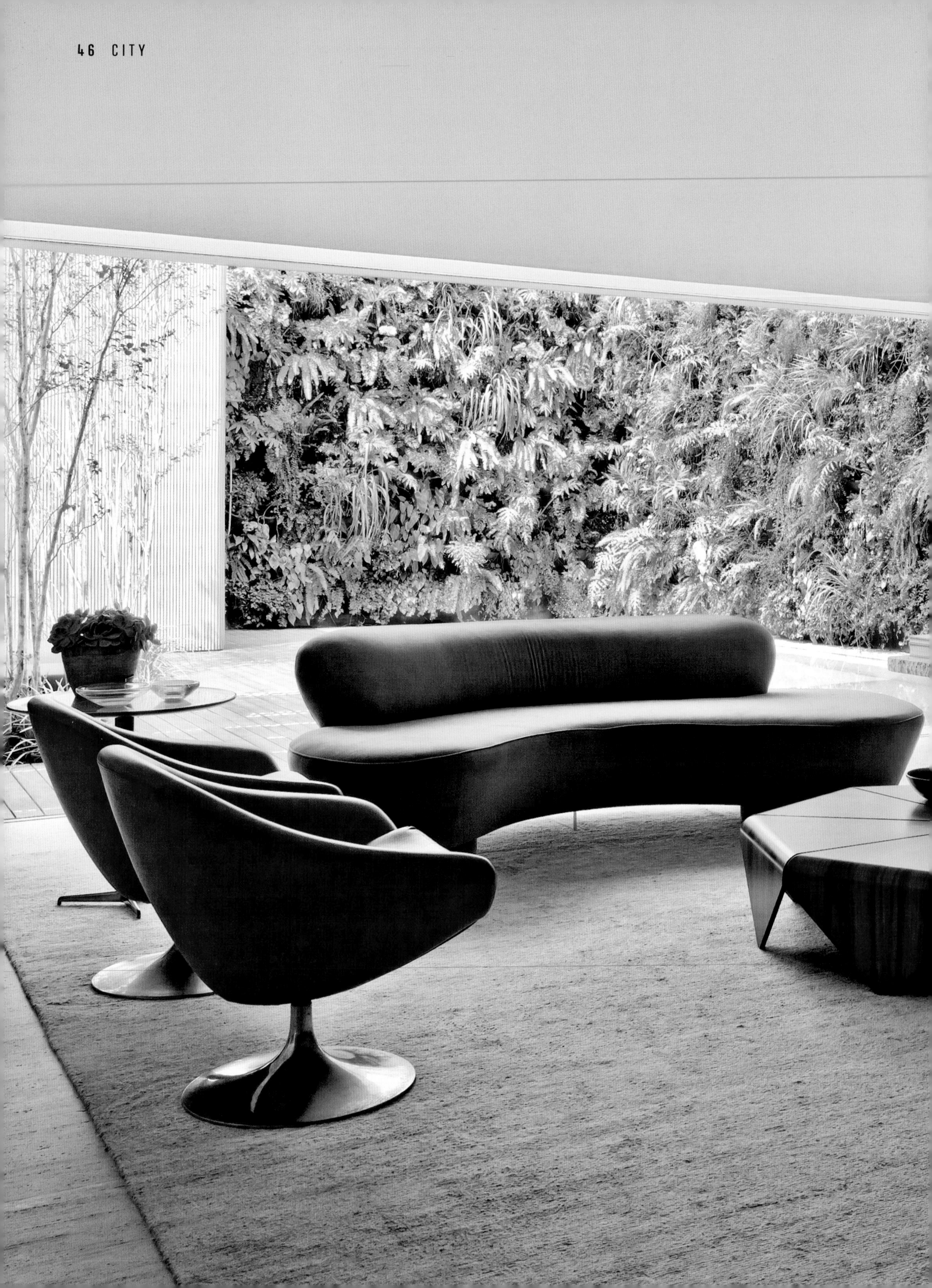

THIS PAGE *Huge glass doors slide away to provide access to the wooden pool deck. Just around the corner, a shady pergola shelters an outdoor dining area that seats ten. The octagonal wooden Petalas coffee table is by Polish–Brazilian architect and designer Jorge Zalszupin, and the round leather chairs are the Swivelling Pod by Overman, Sweden.*

New Paris Interiors

Frank Pont

THIS PAGE AND OPPOSITE ABOVE *The large cylindrical column in the middle of the back wall holds a fireplace with two openings, one for each side of the room. Its gentle curves offer visual contrast to the straight lines and right angles that dominate elsewhere.*

To the left, a broad entryway is dramatically bathed in light from a circular skylight overhead. The front doors swing open to reveal a vast cantilevered slab of American oak that almost seems to float and which provides a division between the three main areas of the house: the living area, dining room and the kitchen and pantry.

The owners love to socialize, so the brief for the living area was to create a versatile space ideal for social occasions. The windows were enlarged and sliding doors leading onto the garden were installed. Outside, a slatted pergola casts welcome shade onto the outdoor dining area, which is adjacent to a wooden deck and the lap pool.

The house has a restful, contemplative quality thanks to its palette of neutral hues and clever use of varying textures, such as the marble flooring, prevents the space from feeling bland. The chunky wooden staircase is one of only a few pieces that were retained during the renovation work on the house.

ABOVE RIGHT *When the glass doors slide open, the vertical gardens can be admired in all their glory. Perfect for a small plot, they provide a vibrant tapestry of lush greens interspersed with the odd pop of colour in the form of a tropical flower.*

PAGE 50 ABOVE *This secondary seating area next to the dining room is perfect for smaller, more intimate gatherings. The Paul Evans glass and metal circular coffee table was sourced at Wyeth in New York City.*

PAGE 50 BELOW LEFT AND RIGHT *The sculptural teak staircase is one of the few elements that survived the complete remodelling of the house. The rich reddish hue of the wood contrasts with the light, luxurious tones of the interior design.*

THIS PAGE *The vintage jacaranda wood dining table is another piece by Jorge Zalszupin, and the elegant three-legged leather chairs are the T-chair, designed by Katavolos-Littell-Kelley and produced by Laverne Inc.*

BELOW *On the mezzanine level, a Flexform sofa offers the chance to recline in comfort and watch movies on the home cinema system. The framed photographs hanging on the wall behind the screen are by Sebastião Salgado, while the cream rug came from Século Tapetes in São Paulo.*

It is a piece of minimalist art fashioned from dark, glossy Brazilian teak. All the furniture, however, is new. Several items are North American mid-century designs, sourced in New York, but there are also some striking vintage Brazilian pieces, such as the dining table made from jacaranda wood by Jorge Zalszupin. 'I wanted the furniture to be beautiful, but above all comfortable,' the architect comments.

The hub of the house is the kitchen, where the owners cook, eat and chat. This space is located behind the steel plate that divides the dining room and the kitchen. On the first floor, a mezzanine level houses a home theatre surrounded by a display of photographs by Brazilian photographer Sebastião Salgado taken from his book *Genesis*. In this bright space, the couple enjoy watching movies. The master suite is accessed via a fitness room and features separate bathrooms and wardrobes/closets for the couple — an eminently civilized arrangement. These small, enclosed upper rooms are all illuminated by natural light provided by solar tubes.

THIS PAGE *This light, bright nook at one end of the mezzanine is the ideal spot for reading the papers with a cup of coffee.*

THIS PAGE AND OPPOSITE *The master bedroom is accessed via a short corridor that is set up as a fitness room. The owners have the luxury of two separate walk-in wardrobes/closets and a bathroom apiece. Their bedroom is a contemplative retreat, tucked away at the front of the house and complete with squashy sofa and giant TV – perfect for cocooning. The large windows mean the room is flooded with natural light all day long, while the wooden screening that covers the façade offers privacy.*

Arthur Casas explains that when he designed the house for the couple, he tried to imagine how they might use every part of the space, and the owner declares that he 'captured her personality' perfectly – her girlfriends say the house fits her like a glove. The owners' original plan had been to move to a smaller house in the same neighbourhood, but after a long search, they admitted defeat and decided to remodel their existing home to meet their changing needs. Thanks to Arthur Casas, the house – and their experience of living in it – has been completely transformed. Despite the confines of the narrow plot, it feels airy and spacious, and the open-plan arrangement of various interconnected spaces suits the owners' love of entertaining.

ABOVE To one side of the pool deck is the shady alfresco eating area and outdoor kitchen. The travertine marble flooring blurs the boundaries between indoors and out. The luxuriant growing wall behind the table is planted with ferns and offers a decorative, ever-changing backdrop.

RIGHT At the end of the living area, large glass doors slide away to provide access to the wooden pool deck. Just behind this area is a shady pergola that shelters an outdoor kitchen and dining area seating ten (see left).

BELOW The lap pool borders the long, narrow plot. Lined with travertine marble, it has a deep ledge all along one side that both serves as a seat and conceals the pool lighting. The graceful forms of trees planted in gaps in the decking soften the straight lines of the pool and deck.

THIS PAGE AND OPPOSITE *The same slatted wood screening used to cover the front of the house casts shade over the outdoor eating area. Made from responsibly grown eucalyptus, it is a strong, dense natural material that's easy to work with.*

A MODERN CLASSIC

OPPOSITE *Designed by architect Paulo Mendes da Rocha, a leading member of the Paulista School, this imposing house is an important example of his Brazilian Brutalist style. A curving stair leads down to the shady pool area.*

BELOW *Besides being a house with great historical value, what delights and surprises is the way that the building seems to float among the surrounding greenery. Supported by four concrete columns, the house has a ribbon window overlooking the treetops of Pacaembu and São Paulo beyond.*

Pacaembu in São Paulo is a pleasant, prosperous neighbourhood. Originally farmland, the area was developed into a garden city in the 1920s and boasts winding, tree-lined streets, large mansions and landscaped parks. It is also home to this remarkable house, built in the mid-1960s and tucked into a verdant hillside. The architect was Paulo Mendes da Rocha, a celebrated exponent of Brazilian Brutalism, and winner of the Pritzker Prize in 2006 and the Venice Biennale Golden Lion in 2016. Having fallen into disrepair, the house was purchased by entrepreneur Houssein Jarouche in 2006 and has been extensively renovated with the assistance of the original architect.

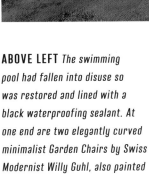

ABOVE LEFT The swimming pool had fallen into disuse so was restored and lined with a black waterproofing sealant. At one end are two elegantly curved minimalist Garden Chairs by Swiss Modernist Willy Guhl, also painted black with dramatic effect.

ABOVE The underbelly of the house. The pillars seen here are two of the four supports that hold up the house. The spiral staircase leads directly to an entrance on the kitchen side of the house. To the right-hand side, the new gate can be seen – one of the few modern additions to the house.

RIGHT The front door opens to reveal the original Portuguese floor tiles – they were chosen by Mendes da Rocha more than four decades ago and seem never to have gone out of fashion. Natural light pours through a glass ceiling.

FAR LEFT With its exposed concrete structure, chunky form and raw finish, the house is a perfect example of so-called Brazilian Brutalism.

LEFT Rising above the city, the house offers panoramic views of the São Paulo skyline. The soaring skyscrapers are a constant reminder that although the house is tucked away on a wooded hillside, it is still very much part of an urban environment.

OPPOSITE AND RIGHT The dining area is positioned at one end of the living space, close to the central fireplace. The salvaged wooden table is surrounded by two different sets of dining chairs, all expressly chosen for the space by Houssein.

Owner Houssein Jarouche is of Lebanese origin and grew up in and around the family furniture factory in the city of São Bernardo do Campo. He designed his first pieces of furniture because he could not find anything that he liked, and his interest in design eventually led to the opening of Micasa, his celebrated concept store in São Paulo. Houssein is dedicated to discovering and showcasing the work of Brazilian and international designers. 'I am passionate about architecture, art and design, and have always admired the work of Paulo Mendes,' he says. 'As I live in an apartment [in São Paulo], I always had the desire to have a weekend house. A friend told me about this house when it came up for sale in 2006 and when I visited it I fell in love. I use it often and it is my retreat.'

ABOVE RIGHT The main seating area is furnished with comfortable, characterful pieces. A shaggy rug softens the tiled floor.

RIGHT The master bedroom is currently in use as a TV room. The battered leather armchair shares the space with a set of vintage plane lockers and an old metal lamp.

THIS PAGE AND OPPOSITE *Next to the seating area is a quiet zone reserved for repose and study. Here, Houssein keeps his collections, magazines and books. The revolving disco ball adds a frivolous touch.*

FAR LEFT AND BELOW
The monumental central fireplace divides the living and dining areas, with its chimney seeming to float above the open hearth. The sliding doors behind, leading to the bedrooms, are new but were part of the original design.

LEFT *The galley-style kitchen is simple and functional. On one side, a countertop incorporates a hob/stovetop and sink, while on the other are the refrigerator and cabinets.*

OPPOSITE *The bedrooms appear to be almost identical, but this one is clearly a child's room, as indicated by the toys.*

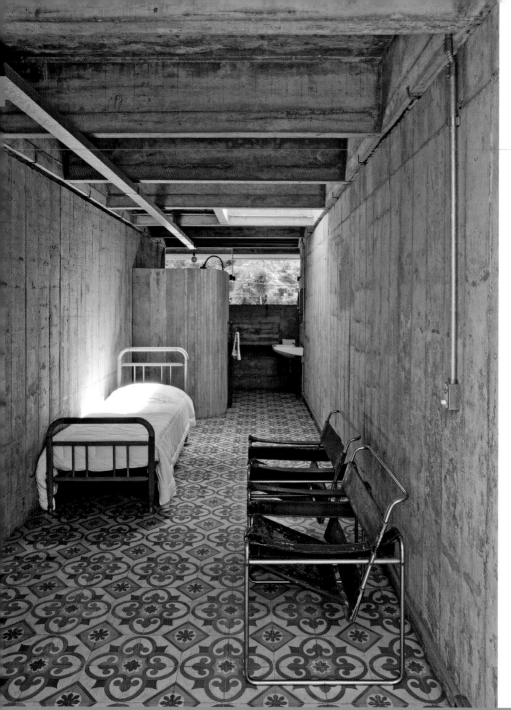

LEFT *The bedrooms are spartan but comfortable, each one furnished with a single bed and its own private bathroom, which can be seen behind the bed. The curved concrete wall encircles the shower.*

ABOVE *This detail shows the pulley system that operates the original windows, designed by Paulo Mendes da Rocha in the 1960s. Each bathroom sports a mirror framed with an old TV fascia, which adds a fun touch to the simple bedrooms.*

Houssein was determined to restore the house to its former glory and sought help from Paulo Mendes da Rocha himself. The renovation work was overseen by the architect Eduardo Colonelli, a contemporary and friend of Mendes da Rocha. Thanks to Paulo, who managed to find all the original plans he had drawn up four decades earlier, Eduardo's restoration was as faithful as possible to the original project.

The house had become choked with weeds and rampant vegetation, so first of all this had to be removed. The reinforced concrete was reconditioned and the house rewired and a new lighting system installed. To avoid cutting into the original flooring, the new wiring has been left exposed throughout. The interior is dominated by straight lines, metal piping and rigid glass and concrete elements, but the original Portuguese patterned floor tiles bring a touch of delicate beauty to every space. The original sliding wooden doors to the bedrooms had been removed at some point and these were now reinstated, while the pool was painted black,

RIGHT AND BELOW LEFT
The master bedroom has a larger bathroom. A long counter runs all the way along one wall and again a TV mirror adds a light-hearted element. The lavatory in this bathroom has a broad wooden door that swings round to screen it from the rest of the room (below left).

BELOW RIGHT The showers are contained in their own concrete pods and feature a bent copper pipe as a towel rack.

FAR LEFT AND LEFT *The spiral staircase leads from the garage below the house up to the kitchen and is a handy way to carry in groceries straight from the car. Another flight of stairs leads down to the lower ground floor, which consists of a small garden, a covered porch, a bathroom and Houssein's music studio.*

OPPOSITE BELOW LEFT AND BELOW RIGHT *The lower ground floor used to be a service area, housing the boiler, electrics and so on, but it is now home to Houssein's music studio. This space also sees a lot of action as a dance floor during parties, hence the spinning glitterball!*

just as in Mendes da Rocha's original plan. One new addition is the gate that separates the home from the street, which was updated due to a need for improved security.

Houssein's second home is dedicated to leisure and enjoyment. The basement, which was once the service area, has been transformed into a studio where, besides producing music, Houssein likes to entertain his friends. The décor of the house is constantly changing, as he likes to move things around and to introduce new pieces into the mix. Almost all the furniture comes from Micasa and was carefully chosen to complement the architecture of the house.

Now all the work is finished and the house sits contentedly on the hillside, its huge windows providing views over the abundant greenery of Pacaembu and the skyline of the city beyond. Supported on four concrete pillars, it is both a piece of Brazilian architectural history and a very contemporary home.

THIS PAGE *The main entrance is via a curved staircase that leads up from the pool. The house is positioned on a hillside, providing spectacular views of roofs, treetops and the São Paulo skyline.*

COUNTRY

BRAZIL IS WELL KNOWN FOR ITS EXPANSIVE
STRETCHES OF COASTLINE AND MAJESTIC FORESTS,
INCLUDING THE AMAZON JUNGLE. HOWEVER, IT IS
ALSO HOME TO ASTOUNDINGLY BEAUTIFUL
COUNTRYSIDE, ENCOMPASSING RUGGED MOUNTAINS,
PINE FORESTS, MIGHTY RIVERS AND ROLLING
VALLEYS. MANY BRAZILIANS ASPIRE TO A RURAL
RETREAT FAR FROM THE CROWDED CITY, AND THE
OWNERS OF THE HOUSES FEATURED IN THIS SECTION
HAVE MADE THAT DREAM COME TRUE.

UP IN THE TREETOPS

Located 210 km/130 miles from São Paulo in the state of Minas Gerais, the city of Gonçalves is set against the panoramic backdrop of the Mantiqueira Mountains. This region is famous for its dramatic natural beauty and is rich in lush valleys and plunging waterfalls. It is a popular area for climbers and trekkers, who are drawn to the high peaks and the well-preserved forests full of native flora and fauna. Renowned Brazilian photographer Bob Wolfenson first visited the area more than 20 years ago. A frequent repeat visitor, in 2011 he found the perfect spot for a home in the mountains: 'I saw this site and I fell in love,' he says.

OPPOSITE AND RIGHT *The house is divided into two sections – an upper bedroom block (right) and a lower living block (opposite). The main living area has floor-to-ceiling windows of tempered glass set in muiracatiara wood, framing the spectacular views and blurring the division between inside and out. Sliding doors open onto various balconies and terraces that offer a bird's-eye view over the valley below.*

ABOVE LEFT AND RIGHT *The two different parts of the house are linked by a concrete staircase rendered in a vibrant shade of pink. The sheet metal roof sits on a sturdy framework of garapeira wood, which was used in its raw state with just a coating of crude engine oil to protect it from the elements.*

LEFT AND OPPOSITE *The separate blocks are clearly visible here, as are the curved lines of the building, which André Vainer designed to wrap around the mountainside. The colour chosen for the house, a rich, saturated teal, harmonizes with the unpainted timber and blends with the forested landscape. The only highlight is the white roof.*

LEFT *The traditional Brazilian fogão a lenha or wood-burning stove that divides the kitchen and dining areas is one of Bob's favourite features – it warms up the whole house and allows for the preparation of delicious meals. A large selection of well-used pots and pans hangs from one of the wooden ceiling beams. The kitchen was designed by architect André Vainer and is made from laminated eucalyptus wood, which can be found in abundance in this region.*

OPPOSITE AND BELOW *The dining table and chairs were made by woodwork designers Mercenaria Trancoso and are positioned so as to afford uninterrupted forest views through the huge sliding glass windows. The unique ceiling light was made from a large fallen branch by Bob's friend and fellow photographer Pedro Farkas. Small drum shades hang from the branch and cast intimate pools of light onto the dining table.*

Bob's choice of architect was pretty much a foregone conclusion. The architect André Vainer was a childhood friend and the two of them had already worked together on a variety of projects, including a house in São Paulo and a beach house. Bob's brief for this mountain abode was a modestly sized space that would be both a peaceful rural retreat and a place where friends and family could come together. And, after working on so many projects together, André 'felt an obligation to create a beautiful home'.

The sloping, densely forested site presented a few challenges, but André came up with an ingenious solution that not only preserved the existing trees on the plot but also made the most of the spectacular views from this elevated vantage point. The house

consists of two separate blocks on different levels that curve protectively around the hillside. One is the living or 'social' block containing the kitchen, dining and living rooms. This light-filled, informal space boasts huge windows and a broad terrace overlooking the treetops. The private block, tucked behind the living block and on a slightly higher level, houses three simple yet spacious bedroom suites. The two blocks are connected by a pink concrete staircase. 'This was a way to divide up the functions of the house, giving more privacy to the residents,' explains André.

The house was assembled using local labour and materials. It is mainly constructed from glass and garapeia wood with internal brick walls and concrete supporting pillars. The sail-like white roof is made of sheet metal, which reflects sunlight and helps retain

OPPOSITE *Next to the library space and the dining table is a cosy seating area that is home to the TV and an open fireplace. The chairs were purchased locally in Golçalves and the colourful assortment of cushions/pillows are souvenirs from trips to the northwest of Brazil, Peru and Morocco.*

RIGHT *Opposite the fireplace, a pair of leather and wood armchairs by Sergio Rodrigues flanks a small table made by a local designer. Simple Japanese-style paper lanterns are used throughout the house.*

BELOW RIGHT *The house is full of personal touches and items collected by Bob on his travels. These wooden handcrafted spoons were made by Pataxó Indians in Trancoso in the Brazilian state of Bahia. The two dishes featuring colourful modernist designs are by Charley Harper.*

heat from the traditional wood-burning stove and the open fireplace. All along one side of the main living block, floor-to-ceiling windows of tempered glass with frames made from muiracatiara wood provide a remarkable view of trees and mountains. Lofty and airy, the house gives the sensation of being embraced by the forest. The teal colour used to paint much of the woodwork helps the house blend into the surrounding greenery and contrasts with the white roof.

The bedrooms are located in the upper, private block. Each one has independent access to the garden, allowing guests freedom and privacy. Bob's bedroom is located at one end and offers breathtaking views over the green tapestry of the valley below. There is a sense of space and tranquility in this mountain perch.

BELOW *The master suite has its own balcony with a view over the densely forested mountainside. Every morning the sun's rays invade the room through the glass windows, which are covered only by a light cotton curtain/drape.*

RIGHT *In the bedroom block, a curved corridor connects the three suites. Each one has a door leading directly to the garden, offering privacy and independence to Bob's guests.*

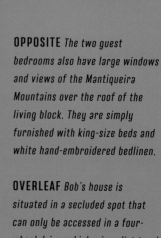

OPPOSITE *The two guest bedrooms also have large windows and views of the Mantiqueira Mountains over the roof of the living block. They are simply furnished with king-size beds and white hand-embroidered bedlinen.*

OVERLEAF *Bob's house is situated in a secluded spot that can only be accessed in a four-wheel drive vehicle via a dirt track road. The mountainous terrain has protected much of the forest here, as the steep slopes make the land unsuitable for livestock or agriculture. As a result, many native species still flourish in this unspoiled valley, among them the elegant araucaria, pine-paraná or Brazilian pine (Araucaria angustifolia). This towering evergreen once covered great swathes of Brazil, from Parana and Santa Catarina to the south of Minas Gerais, but is now in danger of extinction.*

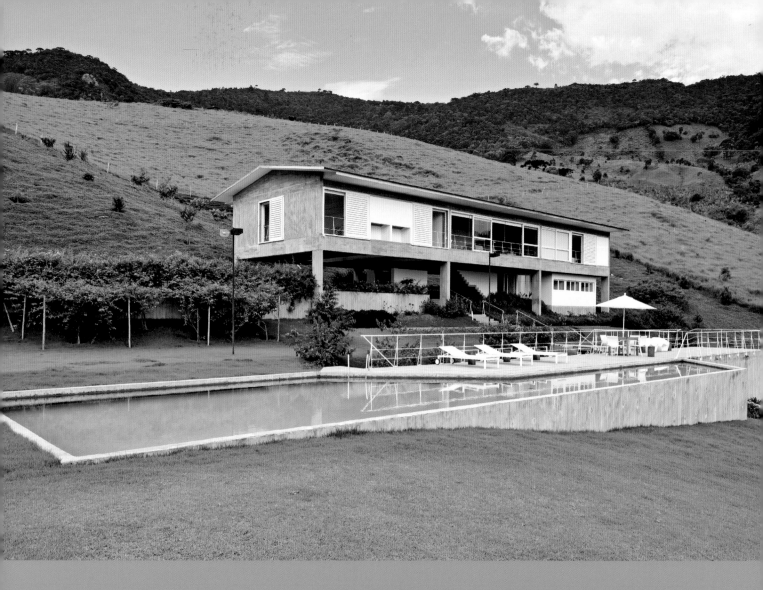

MOUNTAIN HIGH

The city of São Bento do Sapucaí in São Paulo state has a long and venerable history as a religious town. Located in the Mantiqueira Mountains, it is blessed with a pleasant, mild climate and surrounded by dramatic craggy landscapes and rolling green pastures. The area is popular with lovers of adventure sports, hikers and climbers, many of whom come to tackle the highest peak in the area, the Pedra do Baú rock formation, which is 1950 m/6400 ft above sea level.

THIS PAGE *The house is built on a steep gradient and is supported by sturdy concrete piers. A long flight of shallow steps, also made from concrete, leads down from the underneath of the building towards the pool and terrace, which is raised at one end but level with the ground at the other, due to the rolling landscape. A small walkway crosses a drop created by the slope of the hillside. Now the house is completed, the owner has started to plant this area with native species of trees and shrubs.*

The owner of this house was taken with the idea of having a country retreat built on the mountainous slopes near the Pedra do Baú. She wanted a second home where she could entertain friends and family during weekends and holidays and asked celebrated Brazilian architect Paulo Mendes da Rocha (winner of the 2006 Pritzker Prize and the Venice Biennale Golden Lion in 2016) to bring her vision to life.

Paulo's first design was for a tower about 18 m/60 ft in diameter and five storeys high. He planned a garage on the ground floor, a floor of guest rooms, then a large living

RIGHT AND BELOW *The cool, shady outdoor dining area is located under the house. Perfect for family get-togethers, it is equipped with a small outdoor kitchen, barbecue and pizza oven. The brightly coloured earthenware jug on the dining table is from Guatemala. The long table, made from salvaged wood, was designed by architects Beth Forbes and Silvio Nascimento of Studio+ who were responsible for the interior decoration of the house. The colourful rustic wooden stools are from Arte Velha in nearby Taúbate.*

ABOVE LEFT AND RIGHT *A cantilevered concrete staircase leads up to the living room on the raised ground floor of the house. This light, open-plan space is furnished with simple yet elegant pieces, arranged so as to make the most of the glorious views of the valley below.*

BELOW LEFT *The inviting grey sofa in the living room is the Modus by Brazilian furniture brand Oppa; a versatile modular design that can be arranged in numerous different configurations.*

room and kitchen, the master bedroom and on the top level a pool and solarium. However, the owner was not convinced and the plans were not approved. Many discussions later, they settled upon a new design – a long rectangular house made of concrete with a gable roof.

It took almost two years to complete the project. The construction process was complicated and impeded by the remoteness of the site. All the building materials had to be transported via small trucks, as larger lorries were unable to negotiate the narrow roads leading to the plot.

THIS PAGE *The dining table was designed by Studio+ architects Beth and Silvio, and constructed from reclaimed wood. The lightweight, stackable Otta chairs came from the Brazilian brand Tok & Stok.*

THIS PAGE Large glass sliding doors run along one side of the living room, providing views over the pool. The metal trusses that support the roof were left exposed to add architectural interest to the space.

THIS PAGE AND OPPOSITE *A large, modern fireplace is sunk into a raised concrete hearth. The wall behind divides off the kitchen area. The dining table (opposite) is tucked just around the corner, close to the kitchen. The elegant table and chairs are from the Brazilian store Oppa.*

Mark Rothko The Museum of Modern Art, New York

LEFT AND BELOW RIGHT
The delicate metal trusses that support the roof carry the lighting system, while three-quarter-height walls enclose the bedrooms. The monochrome colour palette of cool white and grey concrete contrasts with the rich honey tones of the perobinha wood flooring.

BELOW LEFT *The metal-framed louvre windows are operated with a metal lever. When they are completely open, the fresh mountain air passes through the house and provides a cooling breeze on even the hottest days.*

Almost all the materials were brought in from afar and the concrete for the house was mixed on site. The result is a long, low building that is raised above ground level yet fits snugly into the steep mountainside.

To design the interior, the owner enlisted the help of architects Beth Forbes and Silvio Nascimento of Studio+, both ex-students of Mendes da Rocha. 'I wanted the décor to be as clean as possible,' explains the owner, who felt that the interior decoration and furnishings should not detract from the dramatic

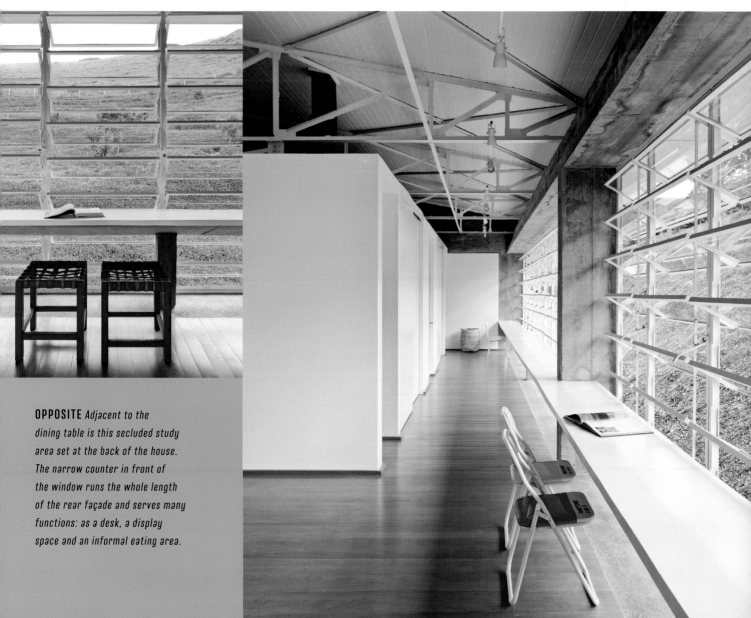

OPPOSITE *Adjacent to the dining table is this secluded study area set at the back of the house. The narrow counter in front of the window runs the whole length of the rear façade and serves many functions: as a desk, a display space and an informal eating area.*

LEFT AND ABOVE *Like any proper Brazilian farmhouse, the kitchen boasts a fogão de lenha – a traditional wood-burning stove (left). This one is, of course, constructed from raw concrete and is faithful to the architecture of the house. In addition to the stove, the kitchen has a gas-fuelled hob/ stovetop set into the long island unit.*

landscape seen from every window. Beth and Silvio were mindful of her requests when they designed the interior. It is elegantly functional with minimal furnishings chosen for their comfort and practicality. They selected a few stand-out pieces, but left the space deliberately uncluttered, allowing the vibrant green of the landscape to become the main decorative element.

The owner's favourite spot in the house is the living room – she revels in the sense of spaciousness and the huge glass windows overlooking the valley below.

'The view from the living room is so beautiful, it's like being in front of a piece of art,' she observes. She also loves the pool area and says that standing on the terrace is akin to 'being on the deck of a ship'.

The house is certainly the main attraction here, but the garden is gradually evolving too. What were formerly bare, deforested fields are slowly being brought back to life by the owner, who has embarked on an ambitious programme of planting native trees, shrubs and plants around the building.

THIS PAGE *The large island unit that occupies the middle of the kitchen was made of concrete and painted with durable white epoxy paint. It houses the kitchen sink and the hob/stovetop.*

THIS PAGE *The bed was designed by the architects Beth Forbes and Silvio Nascimento and is supported on a deep concrete shelf that also acts as a bedside table. No legs can be seen, so 'it's like the bed is floating', says Beth.*

LEFT AND BELOW *The master bedroom has its own generous bathroom. The basin is positioned on a long, deep counter that runs along one wall, while the shower is screened off by a frosted glass door. The view from the floor-to-ceiling window shows the steep gradient of the slope that the house is built on.*

ABOVE *The simple master bedroom suite offers a tranquil retreat from the open-plan living area. It consists of a bedroom, a walk-in wardrobe/closet and a bathroom that enjoys glorious views of the lush mountainside. The grey and white colour palette is subtle and soothing and allows the majestic scenery to take centre stage.*

A FAMILY FARM

ABOVE *An old brick coffee barn or tulha dating back to about 1900 forms the central part of this family home. It sits happily alongside a new addition, a simple, flat-roofed structure built with stones from the surrounding fields.*

OPPOSITE *At the back of the house, large windows overlook the undulating green fields of the coffee plantation. A walkway links the modern block to the original building (on the right), and a wooden staircase leads down to the garden. The vibrant orange clay bricks are the original building material, while the new block was built using a traditional dry-stone wall technique.*

The picturesque spa town of Monte Alegre do Sul lies in the verdant Rio Camanducaia valley in the Mantiqueira Mountains. This is rich agricultural land; green and rolling, dotted with rivers and waterfalls. The region is famed for its coffee production and this house sits at the heart of a working coffee farm. Originally a traditional coffee barn or *tulha* used to store beans after drying, it was converted into a farmhouse many years ago, and more recently, the owner has restored the building in a manner faithful to its original appearance and function.

FAR LEFT *The wooden staircase leads up to the guest bedrooms. The wall reveals the intricacy of the dry-stone walling technique, where each piece is carefully chosen to interlock with those next to it. A vintage tricycle echoes the vibrant red of the wall.*

LEFT *On a wood and leather bench designed by Claudia Moreira Salles rests the original building plans for the house, drawn by architect Renato Marques.*

OPPOSITE *The corridor that connects the original tulha building with the new wing has a glass and wooden ceiling that allows light to flood into the interior.*

RIGHT *Almost all the furniture was made especially for the house, but there are a few exceptions, such as this antique cabinet presided over by a wooden religious carving.*

The current owner inherited the farm from his parents; his father was a Japanese emigrant, while his mother migrated to Brazil from Germany. After they purchased the farm, the old coffee *tulha* was converted into a farmhouse – its traditional brick walls were rendered and new rooms were built onto the simple single-storey rectangular structure. When the patriarch died, one of his children decided to restore the farmhouse in order to preserve his childhood memories and to provide somewhere for the family to gather. Architects Renato Marques and Daniel Fromer of Studio Casa 4 were tasked with the job of restoring the original features of the coffee barn using authentic materials.

When the owner saw Renato Marques's plans for the renovation, he was delighted. But when he showed them to his family, it seemed everyone had a different opinion.

ABOVE *The gap between the two different roof heights was originally going to be bricked up, but during the renovations the architects decided to keep this and other similar spaces open so the inhabitants can catch glimpses of the surrounding landscape.*

RIGHT *The old coffee barn or tulha is home to the main living area and the original clay brick walls set the tone for the décor. Generous sofas and armchairs are upholstered in a simple creamy white cotton and are enlivened by orange and magenta scatter cushions/pillows. The vivid coral curtains/drapes almost blend into the orange brick walls, as does the elegant, minimal wooden furniture designed for the house by Claudia Moreira Salles.*

LEFT *The lightweight coral-coloured curtains/ drapes were chosen to harmonize with the rich orange of the old brick walls.*

ABOVE *This delicate little sculpture hints at one of the owner's favourite hobbies: climbing.*

OPPOSITE *The original coffee barn is now a large open-plan living space. At one end is the sitting room, with comfortable furniture grouped around a broad open fireplace (see previous pages). In the centre is a dining area, dominated by an enormous table designed by Claudia Moreira Salles and made from a rich golden wood that contrasts with the sleek white acrylic chairs. The unusual metal lighting fixture hanging above the table was designed by Ricardo Heder of Lux Projetos especially for the house. The other end of the interior is occupied by a large open kitchen equipped with a typical Brazilian wood-burning stove.*

'It was the thorniest meeting I have ever had!', laughs the owner. Once these opinions had been taken on board, it took two years to transform the old coffee barn to the spacious home it is today.

Renato believed that the building dated to around 1900 and the first step in the restoration was to uncover its clay brick walls, returning them to their original state.

The roof was then rebuilt using reclaimed original clay *cocha* or 'thigh' tiles — so called as they were were moulded on the maker's thigh. Adjacent to the *tulha*, Renato and Daniel built a flat-roofed extension, constructed from stones sourced on the farm and using a dry-stone walling technique that was originally introduced to this region by Italian immigrants.

OPPOSITE AND BELOW RIGHT *The master room was entirely furnished with custom-made furniture by Claudia Moreira Salles. The wardrobes/closets have screen doors to allow air circulation. What really draws the attention is the unusual lamp above the bed, which was designed and made by Ricardo Heder of Lux Projetos. Large windows with heavy wooden shutters open onto the garden.*

LEFT *The wide-legged desk in the main bedroom was also designed by Claudia Moreira Salles and has been paired with a classic director's chair. The striking image mounted on the wall is by Brazilian photographer Feco Hamburger.*

BELOW LEFT *The two bedrooms situated on the ground floor of the new block share this roomy bathroom. The sinks are located in a long, open area, beside huge windows that overlook the garden. At one end of the room is a lavatory and at the other a shower room.*

The original *tulha* is now the social hub of the house, with an integrated kitchen, dining area and sitting room. Large windows overlook the garden and provide ventilation. The winters can be cold here, so at one end of the space is a large open fireplace, while at the other end of the room in the kitchen is a *fogão a lenha* – the traditional wood-burning stove so typical of Brazilian country homes.

The orange of the brickwork provided inspiration for the décor in the main living area, where much of the furniture is made from a light golden wood that is almost exactly the same shade as the walls. The bookcases, coffee table, dining table, kitchen and bedroom furniture were all custom-designed for the house by the Brazilian designer

ABOVE TOP *The practical outdoor kitchen has granite countertops and views over the coffee plantation.*

ABOVE AND RIGHT *The glass side door is one entrance to the house. The red-painted wall contrasts with the orange bricks and the wooden doors (above). The antique tricycle adds another pop of colour and indicates that this is a child-friendly home.*

OPPOSITE *Beyond the kitchen, the outdoor eating area is home to a covered barbecue area with a slatted wooden roof.*

LEFT *The swimming pool deck offers spectacular views over the valley and is fed from a natural spring on the farm. Just like a river, the water is always moving, running in its natural course, so it does not require chemical treatment.*

BELOW LEFT *In a cool corner beneath the wooden pool deck, lush green ferns have started to colonize the stone walls.*

Claudia Moreira Salles, who is famed for the understated luxury of her designs. The adjacent modern block is home to the bedrooms — a master bedroom and children's room on the ground floor, with a guest bedroom and bathroom below. Here, as elsewhere, the unassuming yet elegant lighting was designed by Ricardo Heder.

To one side of the original building is the terrace, where the family like to hang out and drink cachaça, a spirit distilled from sugarcane juice. Behind the house on a raised deck is the pool, which appears to levitate between the rolling green acres of coffee plants and the sky. It is continually replenished by a spring on the farm, so the condition of the pool water is maintained without the need for chemical treatment. The owner hopes that this idyllic spot will provide his children with the same happy childhood memories as he enjoyed.

LEFT *In front of the house, a fountain is also fed by the spring on the farm.*

RIGHT *A lounging space was created beneath the pool deck. A hammock strung up in this shady spot hangs ready for whiling away the humid summer afternoons.*

BELOW *The Monte Alegre region is not only famed for its coffee – it is also known as the São Paulo capital of cachaça. Beneath the house, large wooden barrels of this traditional Brazilian sugarcane spirit are kept in store for big family gatherings or parties to come.*

THIS PAGE *A view of the exterior of the house clearly shows the original coffee tulha at the centre and the new wing on the right-hand side, made from stones found on the farm.*

OPPOSITE *Monte Alegre is famed for its many natural springs and is part of São Paulo's so-called 'Water Circuit'. Its valleys are home to many rivers and waterfalls, such as this one on the farm.*

OLD AND NEW

ABOVE *The imposing exterior of the old coffee plantation, featuring a double row of multi-paned sash windows. The house is split-level, with two storeys at the front and a single floor at the rear, due to the sloping site. Buildings from this era were often painted white purely due to the lack of alternative colours.*

OPPOSITE *The glorious garden at Fazenda Vargem Grande was designed and created by the eminent Brazilian landscape architect Roberto Burle Marx. The work took about ten years from start to finish and the design combines sinuous shapes, stone sculptures, water features and contemplative spaces. The bold planting includes native species from the Brazilian Atlantic Forest as well as imported exotics such as Bombax malabaricum from India.*

In the mid-19th century, the Paraíba Valley, between Rio and São Paulo, was at the centre of the world's coffee trade. Fortunes were made by the 'coffee barons' who farmed the beans and many of them built palatial homes here. However, the boom was short-lived – by the end of the century, the fertile soil was exhausted and coffee production moved to other parts of the state. Many of the historic plantations still remain, however, and the Fazenda Vargem Grande, dating from 1837, is a perfect example of their stately colonial architecture.

THIS PAGE *Despite its timeless appearance, the kitchen is in the modern part of the house that was added during the restoration of the original farmhouse. The traditional fogão a lenha or wood-burning oven is tiled with decorative blue and white Portuguese tiles. The two sinks, one on either side of the room, are fed by running water diverted from a nearby spring.*

Vargem Grande was acquired in 1973 by Clemente Fagundes Gomes, the father of the current owners Maria Lucia and Maria Izabel Gomes. Clemente, an engineer with a passion for landscaping and architecture, faithfully restored the farmhouse with loving attention to detail, scouring historical archives and poring over old photographs in order to return the building to its former glory.

From the front, the house is a classic two-storey residence with arched windows and doorways in the colonial style typical of the days of the coffee empire. Built on a slope, at the front it has two storeys, but at the rear it is a single-storey structure. The living rooms are located on the upper level, while the ground floor is a raised basement. At the same time as the renovation, a new wing was added to the house, in the same style as the original building, to accommodate the kitchen, bathrooms and various other amenities. Today, it is almost impossible to detect where the old house finishes and the new part begins, largely due to the fact that the modern wing was constructed from items salvaged from another 19th-century house purchased in order to provide Clemente with authentic building materials.

OPPOSITE *The back door leads directly out to the vegetable garden. On the wall is a piece of wood designed to hold bananas while they ripen – an ingenious design by Clemente Fagundes Gomes. He was also responsible for the conical light fixtures.*

ABOVE *A side view of the kitchen shows its generous proportions. The large wood-burning oven takes centre stage, adjacent to a long wooden counter for food preparation. At one end of the room, a door leads to a large pantry where pots, pans and tableware are kept. The kitchen has featured as the location for a popular local TV cookery programme.*

LEFT *A Butterfly armchair, designed in Argentina in 1938 by architects Bonet, Kurchan and Ferrari Hardoy, provides an intriguing stylistic and textural contrast with a wooden door that is original to the house.*

ABOVE *The elegantly attenuated lamp with a metal shade was designed by Clemente Fagundes Gomes.*

OPPOSITE *The sitting room combines colonial architecture with modernist furniture such as a Florence Knoll sofa and the Wassily armchair by Marcel Breuer. There are also some very fine antique pieces including the desk in the corner and the long bench beneath the windows.*

Today the sisters carefully preserve the house using techniques that are supervised by conservation expert Toninho Sarasá of Studio Sarasá in São Paulo. The interior retains all its original wall colours and the pastel tones used on the cornicing/crown molding are still intact. The furniture was all chosen by Clemente and combines original colonial pieces with modernist items in an eclectic yet elegant fashion: 'This mix of styles was a hallmark of my father's,' says Maria Izabel.

Once work on the the house was complete, Clemente turned his attention to the grounds. The former coffee yard was transformed into a remarkable modernist garden designed by Roberto Burle Marx, one of the greatest and most celebrated Brazilian landscape

OPPOSITE *An air of colonial elegance pervades the dining room, which is home to an original 19th-century table and chairs. Under the windows is a long wooden bench also designed by Clemente Fagundes Gomes.*

FAR LEFT *On the wall hangs a piece by Roberto Burle Marx and Clemente, made from a casting mould for a piece of machinery.*

LEFT *A small, high-ceilinged anteroom leads to a bathroom.*

RIGHT *On the wall above the staircase hangs a striking modernist tapestry by the multi-talented Burle Marx, who in addition to being a celebrated landscape architect was also a talented textile and jewellery designer, sculptor and painter.*

architects. Burle Marx was an early advocate of protecting Brazil's rainforest and broke new ground by using the native tropical plants of Brazil in his designs – a concept that was to become characteristic of his work.

Water plays a starring role here – Burle Marx diverted the water from the old coffee washer to feed a series of water features and pools. The garden is divided into three levels and includes many waterfalls and water features and two swimming pools. During the planning and planting process, Clemente and Roberto again collaborated closely; the farm's garden is just one of several projects they worked on together.

To keep the spirit of the farm alive, in 2010 the sisters decided to transform it into

LEFT *The house has two adjoining bedrooms with windows overlooking the side of the house, another bedroom overlooking the garden and two bedrooms without windows. The cushions/pillows on the bed are local handicrafts.*

BELOW LEFT *An antique washstand is decorated with flowers from the garden that release their powerful scent only at night.*

a guesthouse, allowing visitors access to the farmhouse and to Roberto Burle Marx's famous garden. This use of the house also generates an income to help with the conservation of the farm. Guests are made welcome by the owners and treated as friends, enjoying the historic house, the extraordinary gardens and delicious food cooked on the wood-burning stove.

RIGHT *This cool, airy bathroom is shared by two bedrooms. The walls were given a special hard-wearing sealed finish called 'barra lustre', which closely resembles marble.*

LEFT *In between the dining room and the kitchen is a long wooden bench with a tiled splashback and ceramic sink. The turned wooden cake stand holds decorative seedpods that were brought in from the garden, as were the tropical flowers in the glass vase.*

BELOW LEFT *A glimpse into the bathroom shown opposite. The wall outside is covered with decorative Portuguese tiles. The large wooden pestle is an essential culinary utensil originating from Africa but which has been a part of Brazilian culture since the time of slavery.*

RIGHT *One of the tranquil, homely bedrooms. The colourful crocheted bedspread and lacy cushions/pillows were made by local craftspeople. The picture on the wall is by Roberto Burle Marx.*

TOP *The garden, created by Roberto Burle Marx, transformed the old coffee yard into a luxuriant oasis with five water features, 19 cascading waterfalls and two tranquil pools arranged over three different levels.*

ABOVE LEFT *These huge grinding stones, formerly used in a cassava mill, were part of one of Clemente's many collections. They were transformed into a sculpture by Burle Marx.*

ABOVE RIGHT *One of the original wooden doors at the front of the house.*

RIGHT *Being in front of a garden made by Burle Marx is like contemplating a work of art. His gardens are living monuments, due to the complexity of their architectural composition and vegetation. The garden's two swimming pools, one for adults and the other for children, are both fed by fresh water from a mountain spring on the farm.*

LEFT *The majestic giant water lily (Victoria amazonica) is native to the shallow lakes and backwaters of the Amazon River basin. The huge circular leaves, which rest on the surface of the water, can reach up to 2.5 m/8 ft in diameter. Its flowers can be white, lilac, purple, pink and even yellow, and open at night only, exuding a sweet fragrance of apricot.*

ABOVE *The original stone wall and metal gate to the farm have both survived the passage of time.*

BEACH

WITH OVER 7000 KM/4000 MILES OF COASTLINE AND
A MOSTLY TROPICAL CLIMATE, IT'S NO WONDER THAT
BRAZIL IS KNOWN THE WORLD OVER FOR ITS BEACH
CULTURE. THERE ARE GLAMOROUS CITY BEACHES,
SUCH AS THE FAMOUS IPANEMA BEACH IN RIO, AND
REMOTE, PRISTINE AND PALM-STREWN SHORES SUCH
AS CARAÍVA IN BAHIA. BY THE SAME TOKEN,
BRAZILIAN BEACH HOUSES RANGE FROM SLEEK
MODERNIST MASTERPIECES TO CHARMING RUSTIC
COTTAGES JUST A STONE'S THROW FROM THE SHORE.

OPPOSITE *One of the two guesthouses. The traditional taubilha or wood-tiled roof ensures excellent air circulation, minimizing the need for air conditioning. The rich tones of the wood contrast beautifully with the lush vegetation, while the red chair echoes the lipstick red Alpinia purpurata flowers.*

IN TUNE WITH NATURE

The sleepy fishing village of Santo André in the coastal state of Bahia is the perfect backdrop for any family gathering. Located on an inlet where the João de Tiba river meets the Atlantic Ocean, Santo André can only be reached by ferry. Undeveloped and unspoiled, the landscape here is framed by palm trees, mangrove forests and broad sandy beaches. In short, it was the perfect spot for Brazilian publisher Betty Fromer to build a holiday home where she, her three sons and their families could spend time together.

ABOVE AND RIGHT *When architect Daniel Fromer designed this house, he took into account the existing trees on the plot and managed to retain every last one of them. He was determined to respect the local architecture and keep any environmental interference to a minimum.*

OPPOSITE AND BELOW RIGHT
*Santo André is located within a
protected area of semi-virgin
beaches surrounded by Atlantic
Forest. It is so peaceful here that
it is hard to believe that the village
is a mere half-hour drive and
ten-minute ferry crossing from
the busy city of Porto Seguro.
Where the garden leads out onto
the unspoiled beach, two areas of
decking furnished with sunbeds
and a dining table provide an
uninterrupted view of the ocean.*

ABOVE RIGHT *The house is
separated from the beach by a
simple wooden fence and screened
by native vegetation. The roof of
the main house is camouflaged
by the abundant palm trees.*

Betty entrusted Daniel Fromer with the job of designing
a vacation retreat that could accommodate large family
get-togethers as well as offering peace and privacy
when necessary. A successful architect, he is known
for projects that combine traditional building methods
with simple, rational design solutions – something
that he learned from his late colleague Renato Marques,
who was greatly influenced by traditional construction
techniques. Accordingly, Fromer chose to build the house
almost entirely from wood. Not only is this material best
suited to the indigenous architecture of the Sante André
area but also local craftsmen are skilled in its use. He
felt strongly that, first and foremost, the house must
be in tune with nature, 'because the environment is
more important than architecture', he declares.

BELOW LEFT *Most of the wood used in the house was salvaged, but the sliding windows were made from certified wood. Betty bought the vase on a trip to Marajó Island.*

BELOW *The kitchen walls are made from burned cement with black granite chosen for the countertops.*

OVERLEAF *The huge modular couch by Estudiobola was the first piece Betty bought for the house, just after finding the land. Her brief to architect Daniel Fromer was to 'build a house that suits this sofa'. He rose to the challenge, managing to meet Betty's brief and to create a holiday home that is perfect for big family gatherings.*

OPPOSITE AND TOP *In the main house, sleek Panton chairs bring a touch of modernity that contrasts with the rustic beauty of the taubilha roof. Some pieces of furniture, including the table and sideboard, were designed by Daniel Fromer and made by a local craftsman. The minimalist lighting was designed by Ricardo Heder.*

ABOVE *The porch divides the living room from the pool environment. The decking is made from reclaimed ipe wood and the roof is bamboo. From the hammocks it is possible to see the ocean and hear the wind sighing in the trees. All the furniture on the porch was made by a local woodmaker. Needless to say, Betty's five grandsons all love hanging out here.*

LEFT *Just beyond the outside dining table is this outdoor sink made of clay and featuring a rustic copper tap/faucet.*

OPPOSITE *The family prefer to eat breakfast outside, gathering around this marble-topped Tulip table by Eero Saarinen. The seats and backs of the director's chairs are made from waterproof fabric to withstand tropical downpours.*

The wood used to construct the house was mostly reclaimed, but Daniel Fromer also used certified wood from responsibly managed forests. The walls are made from mahogany and the deck is ipe, both of which were salvaged, while the door frames were constructed from new, certified wood and the porch roof is ecologically friendly bamboo. One of the most distinctive features of the house is the high, pitched roof, which was fashioned from *taubilha* — traditional handcrafted tiles cut with a machete from offcuts or from responsibly managed

THIS PAGE *The house is completely surrounded by mature vegetation, which provides a sense of seclusion and privacy.*

wood. They allow air to circulate even on the hottest days as well as offering good insulation in cooler weather. The tiles are nailed in place one by one, creating a rustic effect, and should last for 30 to 40 years. When the wind blows through the narrow gaps between the tiles, it sounds as if the roof is singing.

Daniel tried his utmost to respect the essence and natural beauty of this unspoiled place. He wanted the house to impact as little as possible on its surroundings and designed it in such a way that no trees had to be felled in its construction. It is situated right on the water, just a few steps from the ocean, but is screened from the beach by a thick hedge, for the sake of privacy.

There was one tricky issue that needed to be addressed: the lighting. The beach in Santo André is a breeding area for sea turtles

and these endangered creatures require low light levels
at their nesting sites. Daniel turned to Ricardo Heder
from Lux Projetos, one of the leading lighting experts
in the country, to oversee the lighting design. At night,
the beach-facing front of the house is dimly illuminated
by lanterns in order not to interfere with nature.

To accommodate Betty's large family, the main
building is flanked by two smaller guesthouses, each
one containing two airy, spacious double bedrooms and
ensuite bathrooms that are often occupied by Betty's
four sons or other guests. The main house consists of
a living room and a large kitchen, as well as a master
bedroom beside the pool and overlooking the garden.

ABOVE AND RIGHT
*The master bedroom
suite is located
at one end of the
L-shaped swimming
pool (right). At the
entrance, an elegant
colonial bench
provides a graceful
counterpart to the
Spun chair by Thomas
Heatherwick (above).*

OPPOSITE AND ABOVE LEFT
*The two guesthouses provide
accommodation for Betty's sons
and their families. They are located
a few steps from the main house
and each contains two double
bedrooms and bathrooms. The
sturdy wooden benches and tables
were designed by the architect and
the lighting is by Ricardo Heder.*

BELOW LEFT AND RIGHT
*The sleek, functional guesthouse
bathrooms were constructed
from a method known as 'burned
cement', which mixes cement and
pigment or limestone powder to
create a decorative or coloured
effect. The louvred shutters are
made of wood.*

LEFT AND BELOW *The master bedroom has its own spacious ensuite bathroom with doors leading directly onto a private deck – handy for early morning dips in the ocean.*

OPPOSITE BELOW LEFT *The master bedroom suite enjoys a prime spot overlooking a quiet corner of the garden. From the bathroom, louvred doors open onto a small deck and steps lead down into the garden.*

Betty's grandchildren like to sleep here with her when they visit.

All the action takes place in the main house; it is here that the family congregate to eat, chat and hang out. There is plenty of space to relax or to shoot the breeze while swinging in a hammock. The huge wooden dining table is the ideal spot for the family to gather around and there is also a smaller outdoor dining area on the wooden porch where the family like to eat breakfast.

All the furnishings are simple, comfortable and practical in style, easy to look after and able to stand up to sea water, sand and sunshine. All in all, this beautiful and relaxing location is somewhere to feel close to nature and to enjoy the company of family and friends.

ABOVE AND RIGHT *In the main bedroom, Daniel designed a dividing wall that contains a curtained wardrobe/closet (right) and provides a headboard for the bed (above). The vibrant striped rug echoes the lines of the rafters above. It is made from cotton, as is the bedspread.*

NEXT TO NATURE

Santo Amaro, the third largest island of the Paulista Coast, is 95 km/60 miles from São Paulo – a mere hop, skip and jump, by Brazilian standards at least. It is dominated by the busy beach resort of Guarujá, but the tranquil Serra do Guararu Ecological Reserve, in the eastern corner of the island, is home to the Tijucopava condominium. Homeowners here have unlimited access to the reserve, while visitors can enter from 8 am to sunset as long as there is space in the car park. As the topography of Santo Amaro roughly resembles the figure of a dragon and Serra do Guararu is located in the tail, this area is popularly known as 'Tail of the Dragon'.

ABOVE *The house is located on the south side of the Serra do Guararu reserve. The terrain is mountainous here, and the house is hidden among the last vestiges of a mighty rainforest that once covered Santo Amaro and much of the Paulista coastline.*

RIGHT *The Tijucopava condominium complex is positioned above the peaceful, undeveloped São Pedro beach – a popular surfer hangout.*

OPPOSITE *Constructed from wood and aluminium, the house has two clearly defined zones: the private area above and the social area below. The lap pool overlooks the ocean.*

The area is home to the last-remaining stretch of Atlantic Forest in this region, and the densely wooded slopes offer shelter to rare native felines such as the puma and ocelot, while the lush palms house toucans, woodpeckers and several different species of hawks. A walk down from Tijucopava to the nearest beach, São Pedro, is accompanied by a deafening chorus of tanagers and chattering parakeets.

The owners of this sleek beach house wanted a weekend retreat that was large enough for them to entertain family and friends, but not so big that it felt empty when the couple were there alone. Pablo Alvarenga of AMZ Architecture was asked to make their wishes a reality. Since the brief was to build a house that respected its surroundings in the protected environmental reserve, in order to minimize damage to the setting Pablo used a prefabricated wooden structure from the Ita construction company that combines solid timber supports with aluminium door and window frames. This is an efficient, sustainable construction method 'that doesn't distract from the natural beauty of the surroundings', explains Pablo.

ABOVE *The great charm of this house lies in the endless, ever-changing views over ocean and rainforest. The owners love to spend long, sunny afternoons out on the terrace, contemplating the scenery while sunbathing or cooling down in the pool.*

RIGHT *The intricate tapestry hanging by the stairs was made in Iraq and is testament to the long tradition of skilled textile-making in the region. Thanks to its rust and red tones, it sits happily alongside a curvaceous local pot made from red clay.*

ABOVE LEFT *The upper storey of the house can be accessed via two different staircases: one inside and one to the side of the house, offering direct access to the pool should guests want to take an early morning swim.*

The house was completed in 2014. Rectangular in shape, it has two storeys; the upper level is home to the bedroom suites, which have glass doors onto a balcony overlooking the ocean, while the lower floor is open plan with floor-to-ceiling glass doors that slide away to provide access to the terrace and pool area. The décor is simple and combines dark wood and stone with items by Brazilian designers and pieces of folk and indigenous art from different parts of the world, mostly collected by the owners on their travels.

On the ground floor, an informal outdoor living and dining area is set back from the pool deck at one end of the house. Sliding doors divide this space from a seating area dominated by a huge leather sofa that overlooks the pool. A dining table separates this area from the kitchen.

ABOVE AND OPPOSITE

In the outdoor living area, a yellow rug brings a splash of colour that enlivens the grey futon and the natural hues of the rattan chairs and tables, crafted locally from tree trunks. On the wall are two mandalas by Antonio Julião of the Julião Family – a group of craftsmen and artists dedicated to working with wood. Antonio sculpts Brazilian flora and fauna as well as scenes and narratives related to traditional rural life.

LEFT *Beneath the concrete staircase is a reading corner. The elaborate woodcarvings are again by Antonio Julião.*

THIS PAGE *When the sliding glass doors are pushed back, the living area is open to the elements. This space is full of classic Brazilian designs, including the slatted leather Z-Line chair by José Zanine Caldas. The rich brown shades of the woodwork and furniture perfectly complement the jungly greens of the vegetation.*

LEFT AND OPPOSITE *The dining table was designed by Francisco Fanucci of the Baraúna Marcenaria. He named the design Cachorro (dog), as it was inspired by a bench with the same name found on a farm in the Paraíba Valley. The Lapa chairs are by Brazilian designer Rejane Carvalho Leite. The leather seat hangs from the wooden frame like clothes on a washing line, giving great ease and comfort to the sitter.*

BELOW LEFT *The minimalist bar cart was designed by Renata Puglia of the Baraúna Marcenaria and was crafted from solid ipe wood, with trays and wheels made of freijó wood coated with Formica.*

BELOW *The house was constructed around a simple prefabricated structure of wood and metal. On the pool terrace, locally crafted straw baskets soften the right angles and straight lines of the façade.*

RIGHT *Each bedroom is given its own splash of colour and personality in the shape of a handwoven Mexican blanket thrown over the bed. The owner brought them back from one of his many globetrotting trips.*

OPPOSITE *This small living room adjoins the master bedroom. The side chair is a José Zanine Caldas design dating from the 1950s. Caldas was a self-taught designer, sculptor and architect.*

ABOVE *The four bedrooms and bathroom suites are slotted in one next to the other on the upper storey. All of them are the same size and have views of the pool and the ocean below.*

RIGHT *The master suite is the largest bedroom and is furnished with an inviting armchair for quiet reading and contemplation.*

There is also a small snug-cum-television room on this floor. A cantilevered concrete staircase with a minimal metal handrail leads up to the bedrooms. Here are four elegant yet comfortable bedroom and bathroom suites with remarkable views over the ocean, and a master bedroom, which has a small anteroom plus a sculptural freestanding bathtub with uninterrupted sea views.

Despite its striking exterior, this remarkable house does not seek to compete with its spectacular surroundings. Inside, the owners reveal their appreciation of Brazilian design talent and showcase artworks and pieces amassed on their travels. All these elements come together harmoniously to create a home that is all its owners dreamed of and more.

ABOVE *On the upper storey, a long balcony runs the entire front of the building and links the bedrooms.*

LEFT AND OPPOSITE BELOW LEFT *The master bedroom has a shapely freestanding bathtub offering private views of the ocean and the surrounding rainforest.*

OPPOSITE ABOVE *The Gaivota rocking chair is perfectly positioned for contemplation of the restless surf and rugged coastline below. Made from beech plywood, it was designed in 1988 by Reno Bonzon, a French-born Brazilian designer living on the Paulista coast. Despite its sinuous, airy curves, the chair is functional and extremely comfortable.*

OPPOSITE BELOW RIGHT *The tranquil lap pool and the ocean beyond reflect the glorious pastel colours of the remarkable sunsets in this area.*

OVERLEAF *The most striking features of this house are its glorious uninterrupted views of the ocean and the proximity to the last few acres of undeveloped Atlantic Forest in this region. The owners often see tree squirrels and indigenous birds such as toucans and parrots.*

BAREFOOT IN BAHIA

Caraíva is a remote and rustic village on Brazil's Bahia coast, a sleepy spot that was declared a World Heritage Site by UNESCO in 1999. Located on a sandy spit between the Rio Caraíva and the pounding surf of the Atlantic Ocean, this idyllic village is cut off from the outside world – there is no transport infrastructure and the native Pataxó tribe still live here, in a protected reserve surrounded by Atlantic Forest.

ABOVE *The secluded fishing village of Caraíva is situated on Bahia's Discovery Coast. Perched where the meandering Rio Caraíva meets the sandy shores of the Atlantic Ocean and set against a backdrop of verdant Atlantic Coast rainforest, it is a blissful and unspoiled spot.*

OPPOSITE *The exterior of this Caraíva beach house was painted a vivid rust-red shade to contrast with the dazzling blue skies and white sand. The stable-style doors were inspired by old colonial houses and create a friendly, informal atmosphere. The vibrant bougainvilleas flower almost all year round.*

THIS PAGE The sandy soil in the garden means heavy rain drains away swiftly. The native cashew trees were already growing on the plot, while the mango trees and coconut palms were planted later. A shallow step leads up to the deck and, to one side, a small pool invites visitors to rinse their sandy feet before entering the house.

LEFT AND FAR LEFT *The fencing surrounding the house is made from roughly hewn eucalyptus wood – a material that is abundant in the region. The traditional ship's bell allows visitors to announch their arrival.*

BELOW *The broad deck at the front of the house is made from cumaru wood, also known as Brazilian teak, whereas the slatted pergola roof is constructed from treated eucalyptus.*

To reach this coastal retreat requires something of an arduous journey. The last 40 km/25 miles of road is unpaved, so must be negotiated by a 4x4 vehicle, and this bumpy ride is followed by a river crossing via canoe; once on the other side, the only transport available are carts pulled by mules. The unpaved roads are made of sand and illuminated only by flickering torches/flashlights. Although electric light came to Caraíva in 2007, there are no electricity poles or streetlamps – residents demanded that the deployment of electric light in the community was only within private homes, and the wiring was buried.

The owners of this house had spent some time contemplating a second home before they came to Caraíva. The wife dreamed of a remote country house, but her husband's preference was for a house on the beach. While on holiday in the nearby beach resort of Trancoso,

the couple decided to spend the day at Caraíva and immediately fell in love with this charming spot. Together, they found an undeveloped plot on the edge of the village that ticked all their boxes: it felt rural, as it was surrounded by dense vegetation, and was close to the ocean.

The couple had known Renato Marques during their teenage years in São Paulo. Their marriage was followed by relocation to the countryside and the years flew past. However, Renato had

LEFT *The cashew tree (Anacardium occidentale) is native to this region. The open window gives a glimpse of the kitchen with its long wooden sideboard designed by the Studio Casa 4 architects.*

BELOW *The architects Renato Marques and Daniel Fromer elected to use traditional techniques in the construction of the house. The main structure was*

made from sturdy, moisture-resistant paraju wood, while naturally durable golden-brown cumaru wood was used for the deck.

OPPOSITE *In the garden, the architects decided to conceal the water tank in a tower-like wooden structure, with a roof terrace above and a shady deck below for moments of quiet contemplation.*

family living on a nearby farm, and, quite by chance, they bumped into him again. By that time, Renato had become a well-known architect who specialized in working with wood and recycled and sustainable materials and, as such, he seemed the perfect choice for this house.

Renato and his partner Daniel Fromer from Studio Casa 4 wanted to cause as little ecological disturbance as possible in this beautiful and undeveloped place. Accordingly, they decided to preserve the vegetation that already existed on the plot and to use a local workforce and traditional techniques to construct the house, which took about a year to build. All the materials had to cross the river by canoe and were transported to the site via mule-drawn cart. This was something of a logistical headache; much of the window glass, for example, was broken en route.

THIS PAGE AND LEFT *The deck at the back of the house connects the guesthouse and the main building. It is deep enough to accommodate a dining table that seats eight and a squashy sofa and armchair. When it rains or the temperature drops, the adjustable blinds can be unfurled (left) to offer protection from the elements.*

OPPOSITE *Like most Brazilian houses, this one has an outdoor living area that is invaluable in the warmer months, when eating and relaxing outside is the order of the day. Many meals are taken at this sociable square table, while a capacious armchair and sofa (just glimpsed behind) allow for reading or an afternoon nap in luxurious comfort.*

ABOVE *The sandy soil of the garden makes it feel like an extension of the beach. The garden is planted with a mixture of indigenous and non-native flowering plants to provide year-round colour and interest.*

RIGHT *In the airy entrance hall, an antique pedestal table enjoys centre stage. Glossy banana leaves from the garden make for a dramatic arrangement in a glazed ceramic urn – the vibrant green of the leaves really pops against the wood-clad walls.*

ABOVE LEFT *The kitchen occupies one end of the open-plan living space. The lady of the house loves to cook and this area is her domain. It is kitted out with semi-industrial cooking equipment, including a powerful but silent extractor hood.*

ABOVE *During their years together, the owners have collected many pieces of art. These carved wooden masks were brought back from their travels.*

LEFT *From the entrance hall, a door leads to the master bedroom. The simple handle was made by local woodworkers.*

OPPOSITE *In the open-plan living area, the traditionally crafted taubilha roof is revealed in all its glory. The owners love to entertain and this is the perfect space for parties and gatherings. The long wooden table is a local piece from Helma de Itaporanga and the dining chairs are by Brazilian designer Aristeu Pires.*

THIS PAGE *In the master bedroom, the monumental headboard was made from reclaimed wood. It was designed by Studio Casa 4, as were the minimalist wooden stools at the foot of each bed. The bedside lights are by Ricardo Heder of Lux Projectos.*

OPPOSITE ABOVE *The master bathroom has a long concrete countertop with twin basins. The shower enclosure is tiled with glass mosaic in a sunshiny yellow.*

The materials chosen were ones that local builders were familiar with: wood, brick and burned cement. Eucalyptus logs were used to build the sturdy fence that surrounds the house, while the main stucture was constructed from paraju wood, a damp- and termite-resistant hardwood, and durable cumaru wood was used for the deck. The sloping roofs are made from traditional *taubilha* tiles to facilitate air circulation, minimizing the need for air conditioning.

BELOW *This unspoiled village is at one remove from the modern world. Visitors are ferried across the river in canoes, then transfer to donkey-drawn carts to reach their destination. It is all part of the tranquil and unhurried pace of life in Caraíva.*

THIS PAGE *This stretch of the Bahian coast is pristine and undeveloped. A crescent of golden sand stretches into the distance, and dolphins and whales swim in the ocean beyond the reef.*

Tall wooden doors swing open onto an entrance hall with doors on either side. One leads to the master bedroom, while the other takes you to the living area, kitchen and guest bedrooms. A small house that already existed on the plot has been converted into additional guest accommodation, connected to the main house via a wide covered deck. This broad, shady space is an extension of the living area, furnished with a generous sofa and an outdoor dining table. The roof here is made of treated eucalyptus to offer protection against both the fierce sun and the heavy rain showers that are common during the summer months.

The sleek, functional kitchen plays a starring role in the interior – it was kitted out with state-of-the-art cooking equipment and the layout designed for maximum efficiency when preparing meals. This is the favourite location of the lady of the house who, in addition to being a wonderful cook, is a sociable, hands-on hostess.

In the garden, sandy terrain preserves the abundant vegetation, which includes native species such as the cashew tree. In order to create adequate water pressure in the house, the water tank had to be raised to a certain height and to house it the architects designed a tower-like wooden structure. This includes an open-sided deck for relaxation and open-air massages as well as a roof terrace from where, during the full moon, the couple and their guests can observe the village of Caraíva sleeping peacefully beneath vast, starry skies.

LEFT *The materials used for this home – wood, glass and traventine marble – contribute to its elegant, understated façade. The overhanging pergola-style wooden roof creates a long, low line and emphasizes the horizontal.*

BELOW LEFT *The Navajo vase seems tailor-made for the house, with its earthy hues of black, brown and beige.*

OPPOSITE ABOVE AND BELOW *The carbonized-wood effect on the façade of the house was created using a Japanese technique developed by architect Terunobu Fujimori on his Yakisugi House. The raw wood is first burned by a specialist using a blowtorch and then varnished to prevent the colour from fading or the wood from disintegrating. The end result is remarkably hard-wearing and stands up well to sun, rain and termites.*

AMONG THE PALM TREES

Set on a plain between the ocean and the mountains, Laranjeiras beach is located 25 km/ 15 miles from the historic town of Paraty in Rio de Janeiro. The fine white sand here has a distinctly pink tinge; the water is clear and at one end the Toca do Boi river forms shallow pools of fresh water that flow into the ocean. Tucked back from the beach is this house, located in the Laranjeiras condominium complex. The development was begun in the 1970s and is surrounded by undeveloped Atlantic Forest, which is part of the Juatinga Ecological Reserve and protected by law.

RIGHT AND BELOW *The aim of this project was to create a two-storey house that looked as if it was a single storey. The architect raised the height of the house by 1.5 m/5 ft, creating a semi-basement lower level that still enjoys natural light and good ventilation. A marble staircase leads to this lower floor, home to an entertainment zone that includes a home cinema – perfect for rainy days when the beach is out of bounds.*

ABOVE RIGHT *The sculpture is by Franz Weissmann, a Brazilian sculptor who was born in Austria and migrated to Brazil at the age of 11. His works feature a variety of geometric shapes, such as cubes and squares.*

OPPOSITE *The living room is situated at ground level and* *has higher ceilings than the rest of the house. The glass sliding doors can be pushed back so that the room is open to the elements, creating a feeling of being at one with nature. The 1960s leather and rope Jangada chair and ottoman by designer Jean Gillon is an iconic example of Brazilian design.*

The jungly virgin forest surrounding the Laranjeiras complex contrasts with its sophisticated infrastructure: the palm-fringed streets are paved, electrical wiring is hidden underground and the condominium even has its own water treatment plant.

The owners of this house were staying at Laranjeiras when they happened to stroll past a project that was already underway on a beach-front plot. It was exactly what they were looking for and they fell in love at first sight. The house, designed by Paulo Jacobsen of

ABOVE AND TOP *The triangular shape of the swimming pool was determined by the boundaries of the plot. It was constructed from green batu hijau stone with a surround cut from pearly white Fiji stone.*

ABOVE RIGHT *The décor has an informal sophistication that's ideally suited to a beach house. The colour palette combines the warm tones of the various woods with pale marble and grey, beige and navy touches.*

Jacobsen Arquitetura, is arranged over two floors and has a simple, elegant geometric design with a façade made from carbonized wood — an unusual material that blends in perfectly with the surrounding vegetation.

'The great challenge with this project was to create a two-storey house that looked as if it was a bungalow,' explains the architect responsible for the house, Paulo Jacobsen. In order to achieve this aim, the house was raised 1.5 m/5 ft above ground level to accommodate a lower-ground, semi-basement level that nevertheless has access to natural light and ventilation. This lower floor contains the service areas plus an entertainment zone encompassing a home cinema, sauna and gym. The upper floor is divided into two separate blocks, one containing

OPPOSITE *At the back of the living area, an open-tread staircase leads up to the dining area and the bedroom area of the house. The long, low white wall divides the dining area from the main living room space and gives it a more intimate and contained feel.*

ABOVE *In the dining area, the solid polished wood and rattan chairs are the Lúcio Costa by Carioca architect and designer Sérgio Rodrigues. On the wall to the right is an artwork by Héctor Zamora, a Mexican artist who lives in São Paulo.*

an open-plan living space and the other accommodating the bedrooms. Both a similar size and shape, the two blocks are set parallel to each other but slightly offset.

The bedroom block, which is at the street-facing front of the house, is on a slightly elevated level, while the living area at the back is at ground level and so the back of the house opens onto green lawns, a triangular swimming pool and the palm-fringed beach beyond, creating a spacious, breezy and informal effect. As with every condominium, there were mandatory design rules that had to be observed, one of which was that the roof of the house had to be pitched and made from ceramic tiles. Although this stipulation was adhered to, from the outside the house appears to have a flat roof and the sloping eaves are only visible inside.

THIS PAGE *The Rio chaise longue steals the show by the fireplace, alongside photographs by Willy Rizzo and Helmut Newton. The Rio was designed in 1978 by Oscar Niemeyer in collaboration with his daughter Anna Maria Niemeyer. Its curvaceous lines were inspired by the landscape of Brazil and his childhood city, Rio de Janeiro, which gave the seat its name. Made of laminated wood and wicker, it has a black leather head cushion/pillow.*

The décor of this house reflects the owners'
personality, filled as it is with paintings,
books and pieces of classic Brazilian furniture.
The backdrop is neutral, and the white walls
allow the rich mahoghany hue of the roof
and flooring to take centre stage. Natural
materials such as leather, rattan, wood and
steel contribute a rich variety of textures,
while a few colourful details and striking
artworks add personality and interest yet
do not detract from the stunning coastal
scenery beyond the large glass windows.

ABOVE LEFT AND RIGHT *A wooden ledge runs along
one wall in the sitting room and serves as a bar and
a gallery space to display art books and photographs.
The rectangular opening above is the fireplace.*

RIGHT *A long corridor connects the bedrooms.
The doorway leads to the master suite and gives
a glimpse of an artwork by Beatriz Milhazes.*

BELOW *The cosy TV room is located on the lower level of the house. The long, low window is at ground level and offers access to natural light and fresh air. The simple, relaxed décor here features shades of blue, white and beige.*

RIGHT *Also in the TV room, bookshelves contain coffee table books interspersed with souvenirs from the owners' travels, all united by a striking cobalt blue shade.*

OPPOSITE ABOVE *The master bedroom enjoys glorious views over the ocean and the garden, with its lush planting, waving palm trees and velvety manicured lawns. The décor has been kept deliberately simple so as not to compete with the remarkable scenery.*

OPPOSITE BELOW LEFT *The bathrooms are all tiled in white. Carbonized-wood shutters cover the windows and can be opened or closed as preferred.*

OPPOSITE BELOW RIGHT *In addition to the master suite, the house has four guest bedrooms all with en-suite bathrooms. The décor in these rooms takes its cue from the master suite, featuring simple white bedding and brightly coloured throw cushions/pillows.*

THIS PAGE *The large open living room at the back of the house is the only place where the gabled roof shape is visible; from the outside the roof appears to be completely flat. The foundations of the house are made of reinforced concrete columns and steel beams. The main finishes are carbonized wood and travertine marble.*

SOURCES

BRAZIL

Baraúna Marcenaria
www.barauna.com.br
Elegant and functional contemporary furniture designs executed in solid wood.

Dpot
Al Gabriel Monteiro da Silva, 1250
Jardim Paulistano
São Paulo – SP
Brazil
Tel: +55 11 3082 9513
www.dpot.com.br
Modern classics by celebrated Brazilian designers.

Estudiobola
Rua Pres. Antonio Cândido, 228
Alto da Lapa
São Paulo – SP
Brazil
Tel: +55 11 3129 8257
www.estudiobola.com
Elegant, understated modern furniture and lighting.

Estúdio Gloria
Rua dos Engenheiros, 410
Chácara Ondas Verdas
São Paulo – SP
Tel: +55 11 2366 3230
contato@estudiogloria.com.br
Upcycled and vintage furniture. Open Saturdays from 11am-6pm.

Galeria Brasiliana
Rua Cardoso de Almeida, 1297
Perdizes
São Paulo – SP
05013-001
Brazil
Tel: +55 11 3086 4273
www.galeriabrasiliana.com.br
Gallery specializing in Brazilian folk art.

MiCASA
Rua Estados Unidos, 2109
Jardim América
São Paulo – SP
01427-002
Brazil
Tel: +55 11 3088 1238
www.micasa.com.br
Brazilian and international design and contemporary art all under one roof.

Oppa
www.oppa.com.br
High-quality yet affordable designer furniture from a chic Brazilian brand.

Século Tapetes
Rua da Consolação, 3378
Jardim Paulista
São Paulo – SP
01416-000
Brazil
Tel: +55 11 3065 1883
www.seculo.com.br
Classic and contemporary rugs and kilims.

Tok & Stok
www.tokstok.com.br
National furniture store offering well-designed and well-priced furniture and home décor products.

UK

Papers and Paints
www.papersandpaints.co.uk
A large range of paint colours including a 'Mediterranean Colours' chart that contains lots of vibrant, tropical shades typical of a Brazilian home.

Silvia Nayla
109 Westbourne Grove
London W2 4UW
Tel: +44 (0)20 7229 2262
www.silvianayla.com
A selection of contemporary Brazilian design plus some vintage pieces.

The Rug Company
www.therugcompany.com
A huge selection of vibrant contemporary rugs that work brilliantly on stone or hardwood flooring.

Seaside Hammocks
www.seasidehammocks.com
Traditional woven hammocks in a variety of different sizes imported from Brazil.

Winchester Outdoor Kitchens
www.winchesteroutdoorkitchens.co.uk
Emulate the Brazilian lifestyle by fitting outdoor kitchen equipment such as grills, burners, pizza ovens and fire pits.

US

1stdibs
www.1stdibs.com
Online marketplace for antique furniture and fine art offering a wide selection of classic pieces by Brazilian designers including the Z-Line chair by Jose Zanine Caldas and Jean Gillon's Jangada armchair and ottoman.

Espasso
38 N. Moore Street
New York, NY 10013
Tel: +1 212 219 0017
Fax: +1 212 219 0044
www.espasso.com
Modern and contemporary Brazilian furniture including reissues of classic pieces by Oscar Niemeyer and Jorge Zalszupin. Visit their website for details of their branches in Los Angeles, Miami and London.

Restoration Hardware
www.restorationhardware.com
Sleek, elegant outdoor furniture for terraces and decks as well as pieces made from salvaged wood.

Sossego
222 Merchandise Mart Plaza
Suite 1445
Chicago, IL 60654
Tel: +1 312 470 2274
www.sossegodesign.com
Elegant modern Brazilian design, including furniture by Aristeu Pires.

Valspar Paint
www.valsparpaint.com
A huge variety of bold and bright paint shades, from tropical oranges to oceanic blues.

PICTURE CREDITS

All photography by Maíra Acayaba

Back cover The home of Betty Fromer in Santo André, Brazil. Bertoia Diamond Chair designed by Harry Bertoia for Knoll, Inc. Available through Knoll. **1** The home of Betty Fromer in Santo André, Brazil; **3** A house in São Paulo, Brazil designed by architect Arthur Casas of Studio Arthur Casas; **4** A house on Laranjeiras beach, Brazil designed by Paulo Jacobsen of Jacobsen Arquitetura; **5** Fazenda Vargem Grande, a historic coffee plantation in the Paraiba Valley restored by Clemente Fagundes Gomes and with gardens designed by Roberto Burle Marx; **6** The home of architect Julliana Camargo in São Paulo, Brazil; **10–27** The home of Fabiana Zanin in São Paulo, Brazil, renovations by Flávio Miranda and design by Marcelo Rosenbaum; **28–43** The home of architect Julliana Camargo in São Paulo, Brazil; **44–59** A house in São Paulo, Brazil designed by architect Arthur Casas of Studio Arthur Casas; **60–75** The home of Houssein Jarouche in São Paulo, Brazil designed by Paulo Mendes da Rocha; **76–91** The country house of Bob Wolfenson in the Mantiqueira Mountains, Brazil; **92–107** A house at São Bento do Sapucaí, Brazil designed by Paulo Mendes da Rocha; **108–123** A house in the Rio Camanducaia valley designed by Renato Marques (in memoriam) and Daniel Fromer of Studio Casa 4, with lighting by Ricardo Heder of Lux Projetos and furniture by Claudia Moreira Salles; **124–137** Fazenda Vargem Grande, a historic coffee plantation in the Paraiba Valley restored by Clemente Fagundes Gomes and with gardens designed by Roberto Burle Marx; **138–155** The home of Betty Fromer in Santo André, Brazil; **156–171** A house in Tijucopava designed by Pablo Alvarenga of AMZ Arquitetos; **172–187** A house in Caraíva designed by Renato Marques (in memoriam) and Daniel Fromer of Studio Casa; **188–201** A house on Laranjeiras beach, Brazil designed by Paulo Jacobsen of Jacobsen Arquitetura; **202** A house in Caraíva designed by Renato Marques (in memoriam) and Daniel Fromer of Studio Casa 4; **205** A house in São Paulo, Brazil designed by architect Arthur Casas of Studio Arthur Casas; **208** Fazenda Vargem Grande, a historic coffee plantation in the Paraiba Valley restored by Clemente Fagundes Gomes and with gardens designed by Roberto Burle Marx.

BUSINESS CREDITS

The home of Fabiana Zanin
Renovations by Flávio Miranda
Estúdio FM
Tel: +55 11 3042 1007
estudio.fm

Design by Marcelo Rosenbaum
Rosenbaum
Tel: +55 11 3068 0157
www.rosenbaum.com.br/sobre/
Pages 10–27

The home of Julliana Camargo
Architect: Arquiteta Julliana Camargo
Av. Rouxinol, 1041 conj. 1603 Moema
São Paulo – SP
Brasil
Tel: +55 11 5055 2295
jullianacamargo.br
*Special thanks to Alessandro Degano
for our partnership in many projects
together.*
Pages 6, 28–43

A house in São Paulo, Brazil
Architect: Arthur Casas
Studio Arthur Casas
Rua Itápolis, 818
01245-000
São Paulo – SP
Brasil
Tel + 55 11 2182 7500
www.arthurcasas.com/
Pages 3, 44–59, 205

The home of Houssein Jarouche
Original architect: Paulo Mendes
da Rocha
Rua Bento Freitas, 306 5º Andar
Tel. + 55 11 3259 3175
+55 11 3257 8678
pmr@sti.com.br

Renovations by Eduardo Colonelli
Escritório Paulistano Arquitetura
Av. Angélica, 1814 conj. 402
01228 200
São Paulo – SP
Brasil
Tel: +55 11 3257 3620
arquivos@epaulistano.com.br
www.epaulistano.com.br/
Pages 60–75

The home of Bob Wolfenson
Architect: André Vainer Arquitetos
Rua Francisco Leitão, 146
Pinheiros
05414-020
São Paulo – SP
Brasil
Tel: +55 11 3814 8655
www.andrevainerarquitetos.com.br
Pages 76–91

**A house in São Bento
do Sapucaí, Brazil**
Architect: Paulo Mendes da Rocha
Rua Bento Freitas, 306 5º Andar
Tel. + 55 11 3259-3175
+55 11 3257 8678
pmr@sti.com.br

Interior Design:
Beth Forbes and Silvio do Nascimento
Studio+ Arquitetura Urbanismo
Al. Lorena, 937, conj. 305
Jardins
São Paulo – SP
14024-004
Brasil
Tel: +55 11 3729 7189
bethforbes@bethforbes.com.br
silviodonascimento@
studiomaisarquitetura.com.br
www.studiomaisarquitetura.com.br
Pages 92–107

**A house in the Rio Camanducaia
Valley, Brazil**
Architects: Renato Marques
(in memoriam) and Daniel Fromer
Studio Casa 4 Arquitetura + Design
Rua Alagoas, 555
Casa 4D
Higienópolis
01242-001
São Paulo – SP
Brasil
Tel: +55 11 3661 2053
daniel@danielfromer.com.br
studiocasa4.com.br

Lighting by Ricardo Heder
Lux Projetos
R. Fidalga, 563 conj. 12
São Paulo – SP
Brasil
Tel: +55 11 3093 8176
ricardoheder@luxprojetos.com.br

Furniture by Claudia Moreira Design
Rua Pedroso Alvarenga, 990 conj. 102
São Paulo – SP
04531-004
Brasil
Tel. +55 11 3167 6173
contato@estudiocms.com

Landscape design by Roberto Riscala
Rua Arminda, 110
Vila Olímpia 04545 100
São Paulo – SP
Brasil
Tel: +55 11 3044 4049
jardinatto@robertoriscala.com.br
www.robertoriscala.com.br
Pages 108–123

**Fazenda Vargem Grande, a
historic coffee plantation in
the Paraiba Valley**

To stay at Fazenda Vargem Grande,
please contact: contato@
fazendavargemgrande.com.br
fazendavargemgrande.com.br
Pages 5, 124–137, 208

**The home of Betty Fromer
in Santo André, Brazil.**
Architect: Daniel Fromer
Studio Casa 4 Arquitetura + Design
Rua Alagoas, 555
Casa 4D
Higienópolis
01242-001
São Paulo – SP
Brasil
Tel: +55 11 3661 2053
daniel@danielfromer.com.br
studiocasa4.com.br

Lighting by Ricardo Heder
Lux Projetos
R. Fidalga, 563 conj 12
São Paulo – SP
Brasil
Tel: +55 11 3093 8176
ricardoheder@luxprojetos.com.br

Landscape Design by Jose Pedro
de Oliveira Costa
Pages 1, 138–155

A house in Tijucopava, Brazil
Pablo Alvarenga
AMZ Arquitetos
Rua Augusta, 2529 conj. 13
São Paulo – SP
01413-100
Brasil
Tel: +55 11 3062 8699
Tel: +55 11 3062 8330
amz@amzarquitetos.com
www.amzarquitetos.com
Pages 156–171

A house in Caraíva
Architects: Renato Marques
(in memoriam) and Daniel Fromer
Studio Casa 4 Arquitetura + Design
Rua Alagoas, 555
Casa 4D
Higienópolis
01242-001
São Paulo – SP
Brasil
Tel: +55 11 3661 2053
daniel@danielfromer.com.br
studiocasa4.com.br

Lighting by Ricardo Heder
Lux Projetos
R. Fidalga, 563 conj. 12
São Paulo – SP
Brasil
Tel: +55 11 3093 8176
ricardoheder@luxprojetos.com.br
Pages 172–187, 202

**A house on Laranjeiras
beach, Brazil**
Architect: Paulo Jacobsen
Jacobsen Arquitetura
Al. Gabriel Monteiro da Silva, 1310 /061
Jardim Paulistano
São Paulo – SP
Brasil
Tel: +55 11 3087 0600
contato@jacobsenarquitetura.com
jacobsenarquitetura.com
Pages 4, 188–201

INDEX

ACKNOWLEDGMENTS

I would like to say a special thank you to the following people:

Chris and Petit, who taught me my love for books; Ivo, for always
supporting me; Anna, for taking this idea forward; Beta, for the
introduction; the Ryland Peters & Small team; the architects who created
these wonderful houses; the homeowners that opened their houses to
us and to Maíra A, for the partnership and friendship in our path.